NYS Court Officer-Trainee Exam Guide

Christopher W. Brandison

Note: NYS Court Officers start as "Court Officer-Trainees" and after two successful years are promoted to the rank of "Court Officer".

"Success depends on previous preparation, and without such preparation there is sure to be failure."
- *Benjamin Franklin*

"I will prepare and some day my chance will come."
- *Abraham Lincoln*

"Luck happens when preparation meets opportunity."
- *Seneca*

Unless otherwise stated, all passages in this book, including "rules" and "regulations", etc. and names of people and places are fictitious. The author is not affiliated with the New York State Courts.

Copyright 2019 Christopher W. Brandison
All rights reserved.
ISBN: 9781096644897

* = From OCA sample written questions, 2014
(1) = Wikipedia.org

NYS Court Officer-Trainee Exam Guide

Contents

All content prepared in consultation with present and retired NYS Court Officers and NYS Court Personnel.

Court Officer Job / 4
    Pension / 5
    Hiring Requirements / 6
    Salary and Benefits / 7
    Promotional Opportunities / 8
    Examination Announcement / 9
    Veteran Credits / 9

Getting Ready For The Exam / 11
    Formula For Success / 12
    Do's and Don'ts / 13

Types of Exam Questions / 16
    1. Remembering Facts and Information / 17
    2. Reading, Understanding and Interpreting Written Material / 32
    3. Applying Facts and Information to Given Situations / 43
    4. Clerical Checking / 52
    5. Record Keeping / 61

Practice Test Questions / 68

Practice Test Answers / 96

Practice Test Answer Key / 126

COURT OFFICER JOB

The Court Officer job is a terrific and prestigious job, with desirable work conditions, generous pay, and frequent opportunity for advancement in the New York State Courts system. Court Officers are first appointed as "Court Officer-Trainees" and after two successful years are promoted to "Court Officers".

Question: What do Court Officers do?
Answer: According to the 2014 exam announcement, "New York State Court Officer-Trainees...are responsible for maintaining order and providing security in courtrooms, court buildings and grounds.

They work under the direct supervision of a NYS Court Officer-Sergeant and the general supervision of the court clerk or other security supervisory personnel.

After completion of formal training at the Academy, NYS Court Officer-Trainees may be assigned to all trial courts and court agencies to begin the on-the-job training portion of their two-year traineeship. NYS Court Officer-Trainees are peace officers, required to wear uniforms, and may be authorized to carry firearms, execute bench warrants and make arrests.

Typical duties include: guarding and escorting criminal defendants while in the court facility; escorting judges, juries and witnesses; handling court documents and forms; providing information and assistance to the public and other court users; maintaining the security of deliberating and sequestered juries; displaying and safeguarding exhibits; operating security equipment and using established search procedures; physically restraining and calming unruly individuals; administering first-aid and assistance to individuals during emergencies; and performing related duties."

Question: Are Court Officers local or state employees?
Answer: Although Court Officers (NYS) serve in many different local and county courts, they are all New York <u>State</u> employees. According to the NYCourts.gov website, "Candidates are offered assignment in New York City, Nassau & Suffolk Counties, and the following Judicial Districts: 3rd, 4th, 5th, 6th, 8th, & 9th. Court Officers are currently not assigned to the 7th Judicial District. (Cayuga, Livingston, Monroe, Ontario, Seneca, Steuben, Wayne and Yates counties.)"

Are Court Officers <u>police</u> or <u>peace</u> officers?
Answer: Court Officers are uniformed <u>peace</u> officers. They have authority to make arrests and execute bench warrants. They carry firearms and provide security and other assistance in courts statewide.

COURT OFFICER PENSION

Question: Are Court Officer pensions local or state pensions?
Answer: The pension system for Court Officers is the New York <u>State</u> pension system. (Court Officers also receive federal Social Security pensions.)

HIRING REQUIREMENTS

Question: Are there any maximum or minimum age restrictions?
Answer: The Court Officer-Trainee Exam Announcement (2014), does not list a minimum age <u>to take the test,</u> nor did it list a minimum education requirement.
However, <u>at the time of appointment</u>, a candidate must:
- ✓ Be at least 20.5 years of age
- ✓ Possess a High School Diploma or its equivalent
- ✓ Be a New York State resident
- ✓ Be a U.S. citizen
- ✓ Possess a valid NYS Driver's License

Question: My daughter is 17 years of age and in High School, but has not yet graduated. Can she take the Court Officer-Trainee Exam?
Answer: Yes (according to the 2014 Court-Officer-Trainee Exam Announcement.) However, to be appointed, she must be at least 20.5 years of age. (Check the current exam requirements for any changes.)

Question: So, why should she take the exam now if she cannot be appointed until she is 20.5 years of age?
Answer: Past Court Officer eligible lists have been in effect from 4-6 years. If she does not take this exam now, she might have to wait to take the test (in the worst scenario) until she is 22-23 years of age.

Question: I am 59 years old. Am I eligible?

Answer: Yes. There is no maximum age restriction. Also, there is no requirement to retire at a certain age.

SALARY AND BENEFITS

Court Officer-Trainees start at pay grade 16 and promote after two years to pay grade 19. In April 2018, grade 16 starting pay was $49,131, and the top pay for grade 19 was $82,475. These amounts do not include overtime payments, and Location Pay Differential (for New York City-Metropolitan Area, approximately $4,000).

In addition to a good work environment, a regular work schedule, and limited evening and weekend assignments, other benefits include:

- Twenty Vacation days (four weeks) in the first year. For the next seven years, one vacation day is added every year, for a total of 27 vacation days after seven years.
- Twelve paid holidays and generous sick days
- Pre-Tour Prep Leave Time
- Valuable Health Insurance and Retirement Benefits
- Deferred Compensation Plan

PROMOTIONAL OPPORTUNITIES

Court Officers can promote to higher Court Officer ranks and also to titles in the Court Clerk series.

Higher uniformed ranks to which Court Officers can promote are:
1. Court Officer-Sergeant
2. Court Officer-Lieutenant
3. Court Officer-Captain
4. Court Officer-Major
5. Assistant Chief Court Officer
6. Deputy Chief Court Officer
7. Chief Court Officer

(Promotions to Court Officer-Sergeant and Court Officer-Lieutenant require a successful score on a written exam.)

Some of the Court Clerk titles to which Court Officers can promote to are:
1. Senior Court Clerk (written test)
2. Associate Court Clerk (written test)
3. Principal Court Clerk (written test)

(Clerk titles above these three are based on experience, performance and interview.)

Question: Do I lose my peace officer status if I promote to a Court Clerk title?

Answer: No. Senior, Associate, and Principal Court Clerk titles are peace officer titles. However, unlike Court Officers, Court Clerks do not wear a complete uniform (a blazer may be required).

EXAMINATION ANNOUNCEMENT

The examination announcement is published months before the exam date. It contains much information about the job, the exam, and filing requirements, including the payment of an exam fee.

In 2014 the fee was $30. However, the announcement stated that, "Individuals receiving Supplemental Social Security payments or Public Assistance (Home Relief or Aid to Dependent Children, provided Foster Care, or are certified Job Training Partnership Act eligible through a state or local social service agency, or are receiving public assistance from the New York City Department of Social Services) are not required to submit a filing fee. An exception will also be made for applicants who are unemployed and primarily responsible for the support of a household."

VETERAN CREDITS

The 2014 test announcement stated that "Disabled (10 points) and non-disabled (5 points) veterans who are eligible for extra credit will have the appropriate number of credits added to the final rating if otherwise successful in the examination. Eligible veterans should claim the credits when they file the application.

Further information regarding instructions for filing and eligibility is contained in the application. If veteran credits are granted, eligibles will have an option to waive them any time prior to appointment."

Question: If I get a high score, am I guaranteed to be offered a job as a Court Officer-Trainee?

Answer: As in almost all police and peace officer positions, candidates must pass screening checks (background, physical, medical, and psychological tests, etc.)

For current information, see the NYCourts.gov "Post-Written Examination Screening Process" at

http://ww2.nycourts.gov/careers/cot/screening.shtml

The New York Courts Exam Schedule is available at:

https://www.nycourts.gov/careers/exams.shtml

GETTING READY FOR THE WRITTEN EXAM

The biggest misconception about the Court Officer-Trainee exam is that it is a "general knowledge exam" for which you don't really need to study. The second biggest misconception is that the questions are easy. Candidates who are convinced of the correctness of these two misconceptions usually go into the test unprepared and are quickly shocked - and depressed to see the unexpected high level of difficulty that they must deal with.

Because of the difficulty of the exam, serious preparation is necessary if a candidate wishes to score high enough so that he does not have to wait for years to be canvassed for the pre-hiring screening process. On the last exam, this means that to be canvassed within a reasonable time (and not at the last minute before the list expires) a score of 90 or above (within the NYC area) was required. Upstate, the score needed was in the 80s (due to the fewer available candidates).

Our suggestion is that you study as early as possible - and as often as you can. You will notice as you progress through the following pages that by practicing the questions (and using our hints) you will greatly improve your performance.

"They can conquer who believe they can."
- Virgil, Roman poet

FORMULA FOR SUCCESS

First
Believe in yourself!

If you hear a voice within you, say 'you cannot paint,' then by all means paint, and that voice will be silenced. –Vincent Van Gogh

Second
Believe that you can improve!

The will to win, the desire to succeed, the urge to reach your full potential... these are the keys that will unlock the door to personal excellence. - Confucius

Third
Benefit from what others have learned!

Employ your time in improving yourself by other men's writings so that you shall come easily by what others have labored hard for.

– Socrates

Do's and Don'ts

1. Select your study material carefully. Take a look at the contents of a book before you purchase it. The sections of the book should correspond to the types of questions described by the testing agency. If the sections do not correspond, think twice before purchasing it and wasting your time on material that is never asked on the exam.
For example, for the past 25 years, "table" questions have appeared on the NYS Court Officer exam, BUT NOT "GRAPHS" OR "PIE CHARTS". Therefore, purchasing a book with "graphs" and "charts" and with no "table" questions is not advisable.

2. Although it is possible to study even in a war zone - with bombs bursting over your head - try to study in a quiet place where you will not be disturbed. Chances are, you will get more out of your study session. Also, try to study in short sessions instead of long sessions. Try to study every day instead of just weekends. Keep this book near you and refer to it as often as you can.

3. One of the major keys for success on this test is serious and sustained preparation. Therefore, we do not recommend that you rely solely on "cramming" right before the test.

4. The exam admission notice that you will receive from the Office of Court Administration will have the date and time of the exam, as well as the address of the test site. If you are not familiar with the test site or the ease or difficulty of getting to the site on time, we suggest that you make a practice run to the site to make sure that your transportation plan is adequate. If you take mass transportation - or

even if you plan to drive, keep in mind that mass transit schedules and rules of the road, including parking, may change on weekends - when the test is usually given. We suggest that you have an alternate transportation plan in case your primary plan falls apart on the test day

5. The morning of the test - before you leave to go to the test site - make sure that you have the test admission slip, valid ID, at least two pencils (for the answer scan-sheet), a bottle of water, and some quick snacks to have before the test. You cannot do your best on the exam if you are hungry and thereby feel uncomfortable.

6. Make sure that you take a plain watch (not a prohibited "smart" watch that some unscrupulous person might use for cheating on the exam). You need a watch so that you can pace yourself during the exam. Although some test monitors write the time on a blackboard, some do not and leave you in the dark about how many minutes you have left to complete the exam.

7. When you receive the answer sheet, take a minute to note the direction of the answers. Are the answer choices for questions 1, 2, 3, 4, 5 etc. arranged horizontally or vertically?

8. Listen carefully to all oral directions and read carefully the written directions. Even if you have taken many civil service exams, do not take anything for granted.

9. During the test, check the time every now and then to make sure that you are not falling behind. If you have prepared properly for the

exam, you will know that some questions take longer to answer than others. Pace yourself. Make sure that you are going at a speed that will allow you to answer all the questions on the test.

10. If time is almost up and you have not completed answering all the questions, take a minute and answer the remaining questions - even if you are only quick-guessing at the answers. The reason for this is that on this test, you are not penalized for wrong answers as you are penalized on some other exams. If you answer a question correctly (even if it was almost a guess) you will receive credit for the correct answer. If you answer incorrectly, you will not get the credit, but you will also not be penalized for answering incorrectly. It's a win-win situation, so therefore answer ALL the questions. Do not leave any answers blank.

11. If you think that for any question there are two or more correct answer choices, select the best answer and mark you answer sheet accordingly. If you darken two choices, the computer might mark the answer as incorrect.

12. If you finish the test before the expiration of the time allowed, check your answers again to make sure that you have not made careless mistakes.

13. Before you hand-in the answer sheet to the proctor, make sure that your answer sheet is not smudged and that you have filled-in the answer choices dark enough for the computer to scan them correctly.

Types Of Exam Questions

During the past 20 years, there have been usually five types of questions asked on the Court Officer-Trainee Exam:

1. **Remembering Facts and Information**
2. **Reading, Understanding and Interpreting Written Material**
3. **Applying Facts and Information to Given Situations**
4. **Clerical Checking**
5. **Record Keeping**

Each question type has dangers which we will help you to easily avoid. Also, all of these questions lend themselves to being analyzed, so that if you practice, you can improve your exam score.

Read the current exam announcement for any changes in the content or the administration of the exam. In past years, the exams have been in written form. However, it is possible that the exam might transition to a computer exam.

1. REMEMBERING FACTS AND INFORMATION

The first type of question, "Remembering Facts and Information", is usually the first question that you will see on the exam.

At the start of the exam, you will probably be given a sheet of paper with a passage of about 300-400 words on it. (The proctor will place the paper face-down on your desk.)

The passage might involve a description of an incident, or a description of some court activity. (Example: the proceedings of a jury trial, the aiding of a person needing medical attention, other emergency or procedural activity in a courtroom or office, etc.)

The proctor will then instruct you to turn the paper over and read the passage as many times as you want for five minutes, while trying to memorize as many details as you can, without making any written notes. He will tell you that at the end of five minutes, you will be instructed to stop reading and turn the page over. He will then collect the paper and wait 10 more minutes before announcing that you are to open the test booklet and answer the first 10 or 15 questions, and that after answering those questions, you are to continue answering the other questions in the booklet.

This type of "memory question" is asked because it is important for police and peace officers to be able to remember as many facts as they can about people, places and things.

Example:

1. people: Three young men, each with skull tattoos on their right shoulder, were involved in the fight.
2. places: The fight started on the second floor clerk office and continued in the second floor hall.
3. things: The weapons used were two knives and one set of brass knuckles.

This type of question is clearly different from the types of questions you had in school. So, how can you prepare for this type of question?

The following are some suggestions:

1. Read the passage as many times as you can during the allotted five minutes.
2. Each time you read the passage, try to remember more and more details.
3. To help you remember better, try grouping the details into logical order. (For example, group the addresses, the names of people and places, and the time of day, etc. that are mentioned.)
   Addresses: (30 Wilken St., 46 Elmont Ave., 59 Grand Pkwy., etc.)
   Names of people: (Baker, Devon, Jamieson, Martinoff, etc.)
   Time of day: (9:00 a.m., 11:50 a.m., 2:45 p.m., 5:00 p.m., etc.)
4. If you find it helpful, briefly close your eyes after each reading and try to remember or visualize what you have read.
5. After the test monitor collects the sheet with the passage, try to keep the details fresh in your mind. Do not get overly distracted by what might be happening around you.

6. After you answer the memory test questions, do not change your answer unless you are confident and reasonably certain that you are replacing a wrong answer with a correct answer and not replacing it with just a guess or gut-feeling. In other words, stick with your first answer unless you have a good reason to change it.

You can practice the above techniques every day by selecting a passage (about 400 words) from a newspaper or book and reading it for five minutes. After five minutes, wait another ten minutes and then write down as many details as you can remember. By practicing daily, your memory and your approach to this type of question will probably greatly improve.

The following page contains an example of a "Remembering Facts and Information" question.

Example 1:

"Directions: Read the brief story below. Study it for five minutes. Then, turn the story over and wait for ten minutes before you answer the five questions on the following page. Try to remember as many details of the incident without making any written notes."*

The city of Belmontville is located in Dutchess County. Because it is a city with a population under 100,000, it has a single courthouse in the Woodmere section of the city that handles Civil, Criminal, and Family Court cases. The Dutchess County Court is located in the Belmontville Cypress Hills commercial district.

On April 10, 2019, Court Officer-Trainee Janet Faulkner was instructed by her Sergeant to accompany Court Clerk Anthony Begalli who was transporting $15,000 cash from the criminal court in Woodmere to the County Court in Cypress Hills. The bail, which should have been deposited in the County Court had by mistake been accepted as bail in the lower criminal court.

Court Officer Trainee Faulkner and Court Clerk Begalli left the Criminal Court at 10:15 a.m. They used the Court Officer security van. Court Officer-Trainee Faulkner drove. They reached the County Court at 10:40 a.m. There they were met by Court Officer Ben Gardner who escorted them to the fifth floor cashier.

Harold Johnson, a Supervising Court Revenue Assistant, who was in charge of the cashier section, thanked them for bringing the cash bail in a timely fashion. The attorney for the defendant had made the mistake of depositing the bail in the wrong court because he usually practiced in a very small county that operated with only one cashier office for all the courts.

NYS Court Officer-Trainee Exam Guide

Harold Johnson asked Court Officer-Trainee and Court Clerk Begalli if they would wait for thirty minutes so he could collect about a dozen files that needed to be returned to the criminal court. While they waited, Court Officer-Trainee Faulkner and Court Clerk Begalli visited two of Faulkner's friends from the academy. They were both working in Part 43, a felony conference part. During a fifteen minute adjournment of the Part, they all had coffee at Fairmont Coffee on the first floor of the building.

The files to be transported were ready at 11:35 a.m., at which time Court Officer-Trainee Faulkner and Court Clerk Begalli left. They arrived back at the Woodmere Courthouse at 12:15 p.m.

"Remembering Facts and Information: The following questions numbered **1** through **5** refer to the material presented in the Memory Story. Choose the alternative that best answers the question."*

1. The courthouse at Woodmere handles:
   A. only civil and criminal cases
   B. only criminal and family court cases
   C. only civil and family court cases
   D. civil, criminal, and family court cases

2. The courts mentioned in the passage were located in which county?
   A. Duke
   B. Durland
   C. Drucker
   D. Dutchess

NYS Court Officer-Trainee Exam Guide

3. What is the name of the Supervising Court Revenue Assistant?
   A. Anthony Begalli
   B. Harold Johnson
   C. Janet Faulkner
   D. George Jamison

4. The number of the Part where the Court-Officer Trainee's two friends worked was:
   A. Part 34
   B. Part 53
   C. Part 43
   D. Part 32

5. The files to be transported were ready at _____.
   A. 11:35 a.m.
   B. 12:15 p.m.
   C. 11:53 a.m.
   D. 11: 25 a.m.

Answers 1 - 5

1. D. civil, criminal, and family court cases: "...a single courthouse in the Woodmere section of the city that handles Civil, Criminal, and Family Court cases."

2. D. Dutchess: "The city of Belmontville is locate in Dutchess County...The county court is located in the Cypress Hills commercial district.

NYS Court Officer-Trainee Exam Guide

3. **B. Harold Johnson:** "Harold Johnson, a Supervising Court Revenue Assistant, who was in charge of the cashier section, thanked them for bringing the cash bail in a timely fashion."

4. **C. Part 43:** "They were both working in Part 43, a felony conference part."

5. **A. 11:35 a.m.:** "The files to be transported were ready at 11:35 a.m."

Let's try another example:

Example 2:
"Directions: Read the brief story below. Study it for five minutes. Then, turn the story over and wait for ten minutes before you answer the five questions (6-10) on the following page. Try to remember as many details of the incident without making any written notes."*

On Tuesday, December 3, 2019, at 9:15 a.m., Court Officer-Trainee Carole Simmons reported to Civil Court Part 16, where a jury trial was scheduled to begin that day. She was filling-in for Court Officer Harold Wilkison who was out because he was a subpoenaed witness in an auto accident case in Part 19.

A few minutes later, the second Court Officer assigned to the Part, Robert Patronich, arrived, along with eight jurors who had been selected the day before. Six of the jurors formed the regular jury and two jurors were designated as alternate jurors.

The Judge in the Part, Judge Manuel Fernandez, arrived at 9:30 a.m. After all the parties and their attorneys arrived, the Judge held a conference with the attorneys in a side room. At 10:00 a.m. the trial began. After some introductory remarks by the Judge to the jury, the plaintiff's attorney delivered opening statements, followed by opening statements by the defendant's attorney.

During the remainder of the morning session, the plaintiff and another witness gave testimony. In the afternoon, three witnesses gave testimony. At 4:00 p.m., after all the witnesses for the day had testified, the Judge asked both attorneys to participate in a settlement conference outside the view of the jury. During the conference, the defendant's attorney offered to settle the case for $85,000, however the attorney for the plaintiff demanded $150,000. After much discussion, the Judge suggested a settlement amount of $125,000. He stated to both attorneys that he thought this was a fair amount, based on the strength of the plaintiff's testimony and the likelihood that the plaintiff would be awarded at least that much by the jury.

The plaintiff and his attorney were agreeable to the $125,000 settlement amount. However, since the attorney for the defendant was there in behalf of the defendant and the defendant's insurance company, he suggested a quick break so he could convey the offer to the insurance company's legal office. Fifteen minutes later, the attorney for the defendant reported that the offer was acceptable to the insurance company.

By 4:55 p.m., the settlement had been recorded on the record and the jury had been thanked by the Judge and dismissed.

NYS Court Officer-Trainee Exam Guide

"**Remembering Facts and Information:** The following questions numbered **6** through **10** refer to the material presented in the Memory Story. Choose the alternative that best answers the question."*

6. The Part to which Court Officer-Trainee Carole Simmons was assigned is _____.
   A. Part 6
   B. Part 16
   C. Part 9
   D. Part 19

7. The name of the Judge in the part where Court Officer-Trainee Simmons was assigned is _____.
   A. Judge Manuel Fernandez
   B. Judge Manuel Hernandes
   C. Judge Manel Fernandez
   D. Judge Mannuel Fernandez

8. The trial began at _____.
   A. 9:00 a.m.
   B. 9:15 a.m.
   C. 9:30 a.m.
   D. 10:00 a.m.

9. Total number of witnesses that testified during the day was _____.
   A. 2
   B. 5
   C. 3
   D. 4

10. The final settlement amount was _____.
   A. $150,000
   B. $125,000
   C. $95,000
   D. $135,000

Answers 6 - 10

6. B. Part 16: "On Tuesday, December 3, 2019, at 9:15 a.m., Court Officer-Trainee Carole Simmons reported to Civil Court Part 16.

7. A. Judge Manuel Fernandez: "The Judge in the Part, Judge Manuel Fernandez, arrived at 9:30 a.m."

8. D. 10:00 a.m.: "At 10:00 a.m. the trial began."

9. B. 5: "During the remainder of the morning session, the plaintiff and another witness gave testimony. In the afternoon, three witnesses gave testimony."

10. B. $125,000: "...the Judge suggested a settlement amount of $125,000... Fifteen minutes later, the attorney for the defendant reported that the offer was acceptable to the insurance company."

Example 3:

"Directions: Read the brief story below. Study it for five minutes. Then, turn the story over and wait for ten minutes before you answer the ten questions (11-20) on the following page. Try to remember as many details of the incident without making any written notes."*

On Monday morning, at 9:00 a.m., the street outside the criminal court building in Bronx County buzzed with activity with two opposing demonstrations of more than 100 demonstrators each. Jane Newfeld, a Court Officer-Trainee, was assigned in front of the court building, along with three other Court Officer-Trainees, Court Officer-Sergeant Manitello and Court Officer-Lieutenant Osborne.

The leader of one of the demonstrations chanted "Let Harry Winston go!" while the leader of the opposing demonstration chanted, "Lock him up - throw away the key!" Court Officer-Trainee Newfeld's assignment was to stay close to George Becker, the leader of the "Let Harry Winston go!" faction. Earlier in the morning he had reported to Major Richards that during the night he had received two death threats by phone.

For a couple of hours, there was a great deal of chanting and marching up and down the sidewalks, but no violence. However, at 11:05 a.m. two male demonstrators, one from each faction got into a violent fist fight. Court Officers quickly surrounded them and broke up the fight. Each of the two men complained that the other person started the fight by "spitting first."

As the two men were being questioned, Court Officer-Trainee Verna Holmes noticed a knife falling out of the back pocket of one of the men. She quickly realized that it was a switchblade knife, illegal under the Penal Code. Lieutenant Osborne instructed Court Officer-Trainee Holmes to take the person under custody. The other person was also taken into custody, as he was found by Court Officer-Trainee Brenda Fullman, to be in possession of metal knuckles.

The demonstrations continued until 2:07 p.m., when news arrived that the case had been adjourned until the following day. All the officers were relieved that for the day at least the excitement was over. However, Court Officer-Lieutenant Osborne, advised all of them to get some lunch and then some rest, because he had been informed by both demonstration leaders that everyone would be back the following morning.

"**Remembering Facts and Information:** The following questions numbered **11** through **20** refer to the material presented in the preceding Memory Story. Select the choice that best answers the question."*

11. The demonstration continued until _____.
A. 12:09 p.m.
B. 3:07 p.m.
C. 2:09 p.m.
D. 2:07 p.m.

12. The rank of Court Officer Osborne is _____.
A. Major
B. Lieutenant
C. Sergeant
D. Court Officer-Trainee

13. Which Court Officer first noticed the knife?
A. Court Officer-Trainee Thelma Lomes
B. Court Officer-Trainee Vilma Thomes
C. Court Officer-Trainee Verna Holmes
D. Court Officer-Trainee Mera Gomez

14. What kind of knife was discovered?

A. cutting knife

B. two edged kitchen knife

C. baruko knife

D. switchblade knife

15. The criminal court where the demonstrations occurred is in _____ County.

A. Queens

B. Bronx

C. Queens

D. New York

16. _____ Newfeld, a Court Officer-Trainee was assigned in front of the court building.

A. Jean

B. Jane

C. Janie

D. Janey

17. The total number of Court Officer-Trainees assigned outside the court building was _____.

A. two

B. three

C. four

D. five

NYS Court Officer-Trainee Exam Guide

18. What is the name of the leader of the ""Let Harry Winston go!" faction?

A. George Manitello

B. George Winston

C. George Holmes

D. George Becker

19. The last name of the Major is _____.

A. Holmes

B. Richards

C. Osborne

D. Newfeld

20. At what time did the two demonstrators get into a fight?

A. 9:00 a.m.

B. 11:05 a.m.

C. 10:05 a.m.

D. 12:05 a.m.

Answers 11-20

11. D. 2:07 p.m.: "The demonstrations continued until **2:07 p.m.**, when news arrived that the case had been adjourned until the following day."

12. B. Lieutenant: "However, Court Officer-Lieutenant Osborne, advised all of them to...."

13. C. Court Officer-Trainee Verna Holmes: "Court Officer-Trainee Verna Holmes noticed a knife falling out of the back pocket...."

14. D. switchblade knife: " She quickly realized that it was a switchblade knife...."

15. B. Bronx: "... the street outside the criminal court building in Bronx County buzzed with activity."

16. B. Jane: "Jane Newfeld, a Court Officer-Trainee was assigned in front of the court building."

17. C. four: "Jane Newfeld, a Court Officer-Trainee was assigned in front of the court building, along with three other Court Officer-Trainees."

18. D. George Becker: "... George Becker, the leader of the 'Let Harry Winston go!' faction."

19. B. Richards: "Earlier in the morning he had reported to Major Richards that during the night he had received two death threats by phone."

20. B. 11:05 a.m.: "However, at 11:05 a.m. two male demonstrators, one from each faction got into a violent fist fight."

2. READING, UNDERSTANDING AND INTERPRETING WRITTEN MATERIAL (2 DIFFERENT QUESTION TYPES)

"This section of the written exam assesses your ability to read and understand written material. There are two ways (formats) contained in the test which are used to measure your reading ability. You should familiarize yourself with each of the two formats.

FORMAT A

In this format, each question contains a brief reading selection followed by a question or questions pertaining to the information in the selection. All of the information required to answer the question(s) is provided, so even if the reading selection is on a topic with which you are not familiar, you will be able to answer the question(s) by reading the selection carefully. Remember, answer the questions based only on the information you read in the selection. Do not use any prior knowledge that you may have on the subject in choosing your answers."*

"Directions: After reading the selection below, choose the alternative which best answers the question following the selection."*

"New York State Court Officers are New York State peace officers authorized to execute bench warrants in and about courthouses, make arrests both on and off duty, issue summonses for penal law violations, parking and moving infractions and use physical and deadly force....New York State Court Officers are authorized to carry firearms, expandable baton, handcuffs, flashlight, bullet resistant vest, pepper spray, and a radio that is directly linked to other officers....New York State Court Officers undergo comprehensive basic training at the NYS Court Officers Academy which was founded by Chief Thomas R. Hennessy (Ret.) The curriculum includes but is not limited to training in criminal and civil procedure law, constitutional law, stop and frisk, search and seizure, police science, laws of arrest, use of physical and deadly physical force, firearms training, situation and judgment, defensive tactics, tactical communication, arrest procedures, gang intelligence and first aid/cpr/basic life support. Chief Joseph Baccellieri, Jr. is the Chief of Training throughout the state and the Commanding Officer of the Academy".(1)

1. According to the preceding passage, which of the following four statements is most correct?
    A. The curriculum includes training in family court law.
    B. Chief Thomas R. Hennessey is the Chief Training Officer.
    C. Court Officers are not authorized to carry pepper spray.
    D. Gang intelligence is a part of the curriculum.

Answer questions 2 and 3 based on the following passage.

"The purpose of fire drills in buildings is to ensure that everyone knows how to exit safely as quickly as possible if a fire, smoke, carbon monoxide or other emergency occurs. People need to recognize the sound of the fire alarm.

Before regular fire drills were instituted, a fire that had a major impact broke out at the private Catholic school Our Lady of the Angels in 1958, in Chicago, Illinois, US. Children on the second floor were trapped there, with neither teachers nor pupils knowing how to get out of the building safely. Many children jumped out of windows, and many were killed as they could not make their way to an exit. Although the school had passed a fire inspection two months before, and had the number of fire exits and fire extinguishers required at the time, it lacked smoke detectors or adequate fire alarms, and was overcrowded.

The need for fire drills was recognized; monthly fire drills were put in place after the Our Lady of the Angels fire. It was found in a later study that education on fire also helped to prevent it: people started to learn more about what started fires, and what to do in the case of one starting. They were also aware of the hazards that allow a fire to start. Within a year of the fire, many of the hazardous conditions found in Our Lady of the Angels had been eliminated in thousands of schools around the United States."[1]

2. According to the preceding passage, which of the following four statements is correct?
   A. Quarterly fire drills were put in place after the Our Lady of the Angels fire.
   B. Our Lady of the Angels is located in Chicago, Indiana.
   C. The school had passed a fire inspection two months before.
   D. The exclusive purpose of fire drills in buildings is to ensure that everyone knows how to exit safely as quickly as possible if a fire, smoke, or carbon monoxide emergency occurs.

3. Which of the following four statements is supported by the preceding passage?

   A. Education on fire does not help to prevent it.

   B. Fire drills cause fires.

   C. Our Lady of Angels had not been inspected for three months.

   D. Our Lady of Angels was overcrowded. /

Answer questions 4 and 5 based on the following passage.

"The court of general jurisdiction in New York is the New York Supreme Court. (Unlike in most other states, the Supreme Court is a trial court and is not the highest court in the state.) There is a branch of the New York Supreme Court in each of New York State's 62 counties.

In New York City, the Supreme Court in each county hears all felony cases; outside New York City, these cases are generally heard in the County Court. The Supreme Court hears civil cases seeking money damages that exceed the monetary limits of the local courts' jurisdiction. The Supreme Court has exclusive jurisdiction over most cases in which a party seeks equitable relief such as an injunction, declaratory judgment actions, or proceedings for review of many administrative-agency rulings. The court also has exclusive jurisdiction over matrimonial actions seeking a divorce, legal separation, or annulment of a marriage. In several counties the Supreme Court has a specialized Commercial Division that hears commercial cases.

The New York State County Court operates in each county except for the five counties of New York City (in those counties, the Civil Court, Criminal Court and Supreme Court operate in place of a typical County Court). In many counties, this court primarily hears criminal cases (whereas the Supreme Court primarily hears civil cases), and usually only felonies, as lesser crimes are handled by local courts."(1)

4. According to the preceding passage, which of the following four statements is correct?
   A. The courts in NYS are the same in each county of the state.
   B. The Supreme Court primarily hears criminal cases.
   C. Each county in NYS has a Supreme Court.
   D. The District Court has exclusive jurisdiction over all cases.

5. According to the preceding passage, which of the following four statements is correct?
   A. The Supreme Court is the highest court in the state.
   B. The Supreme Court is an appellate court, and not a trial court.
   C. The Supreme Court does not have jurisdiction over legal separation.
   D. The Supreme Court Commercial Division is found in several counties.

Answers 1-5

1. **D. Gang intelligence is a part of the curriculum:** "The curriculum includes...gang intelligence...."
   Choice "A" is not correct because "The curriculum includes but is not limited to training in criminal and civil procedure law "

Choice "B" is not correct because "Chief Joseph Baccellieri, Jr. is the Chief of Training throughout the state and the Commanding Officer of the Academy.

Choice "C" is not correct because they <u>are</u> authorized to carry pepper spray, "New York State Court Officers are authorized to carry firearms, expandable baton, handcuffs, flashlight, bullet resistant vest, <u>pepper spray</u>."

2. C. The school had passed a fire inspection two months before.
This is the answer because this is the only statement that is correct. The passage clearly states that ".. the school had passed a fire inspection two months before."
Choice "A" is not correct because <u>monthly</u> and not quarterly fire drills were put in place.
Choice "B" is not correct because "... Our Lady of the Angels in 1958, in Chicago, <u>Illinois</u>." (not Indiana)
Choice "D" is not correct because "The purpose of fire drills in buildings is to ensure that everyone knows how to exit safely as quickly as possible if a fire, smoke, carbon monoxide <u>or other emergency occurs</u>."

3. D. Our Lady of Angels was overcrowded: "Although the school had passed a fire inspection two months before, and had the number of fire exits and fire extinguishers required at the time, it lacked smoke detectors or adequate fire alarms, and <u>was overcrowded</u>."
Choice "A" is not correct because "It was found in a later study that education on fire also <u>helped to prevent it</u>."

Choice "B" is not correct because "...education on fire also helped to prevent it."

Choice "C" is not correct because "...the school had passed a fire inspection <u>two</u> months before...."

4. **C. Each county in NYS has a Supreme Court:** "There is a branch of the New York Supreme Court in each of New York State's 62 counties."

   Choice "A" is not correct because " The New York State County Court operates in each county <u>except</u> for the five counties of New York City (in those counties, the Civil Court, Criminal Court and Supreme Court operate in place of a typical County Court).

   Choice "B" is not correct because "The Supreme Court hears <u>civil</u> cases seeking money damages that exceed the monetary limits of the local courts' jurisdiction."

   Choice "D" is not correct because the passage does not mention District Courts.

5. **D. The Supreme Court Commercial Division is found in several counties:** "In several counties the Supreme Court has a specialized Commercial Division that hears commercial cases."

   Choice "A" is not correct because the passage does not state this. (The highest court in the state is the Court of Appeals.)

   Choice "B" is not correct because, for example: "In New York City, the Supreme Court in each county hears all felony cases." (It is a <u>trial</u> court.)

   Choice "C" is not correct because "The court also has exclusive jurisdiction over matrimonial actions seeking a divorce, <u>legal separation</u>, or annulment of a marriage."

FORMAT B

"In this format the test contains a short, written passage from which some words have been omitted. You need to select one word from the four alternatives that best completes the passage."*

"Directions: The three passages below each contain five numbered blanks. Below each passage are listed five sets of words numbered to match the blanks. Pick the word from each set which seems to make the most sense both in the sentence and the total paragraph."*

Passage 1

"Physical ____1____ such as fences, walls, and vehicle barriers act as the outermost layer of security. They serve to prevent, or at least ____2____, attacks, and also act as a psychological deterrent by defining the perimeter of the facility and making intrusions seem ____3____ difficult. Tall fencing, topped with barbed wire, razor wire or metal spikes are often placed on the ____4____ of a property, generally with some type of signage that warns people not to attempt to enter. However, in some ____5____ imposing perimeter walls/fencing will not be possible (e.g. an urban office building that is directly adjacent to public sidewalks) or it may be aesthetically unacceptable."(1)

1.	2.	3.	4.	5.
a. portal	a. advance	a. less	a. center	a. facilliies
b. barriers	b. aid	b. not	b. perimeter	b. facilities
c. entry	c. delay	c. negligible	c. middle	c. faccilities
d. pass	d. help	d. more	d. nucleus	d. facelities

NYS Court Officer-Trainee Exam Guide

Passage 2

"Crowd control is ____6____ public security practice where large crowds are managed to prevent the outbreak of crowd crushes, affray, fights involving drunk and disorderly people or riots. Crowd crushes in particular can cause many ____7____ of fatalities. Effective crowd management is about ____8____ expected and unexpected ____9____ occurrences. Crowd control can involve privately hired security guards as well as police officers. Crowd control is often used at large, public ____10____ like street fairs, music festivals, stadiums and public demonstrations. At some events, security guards and police use metal detectors and sniffer dogs to prevent weapons and drugs being brought into a venue."(1)

6.	7.	8.	9.	10.
a. several	a. few	a. manageing	a. sedate	a. scattering
b. many	b. hundreds	b. mannaging	b. ordinary	b. gathering
c. a	c. ten	c. managing	c. calm	c. imaginary
d. two	d. hundred	d. maneging	d. crowd	d. gatherings

Passage 3

"____11____ opening statement is generally the first occasion that the trier of fact (jury or judge) has to hear from a lawyer in a trial, aside possibly from questioning during voir dire. The opening statement is generally ____12____ to serve as a "road map" for the fact-finder. This is especially essential, in many jury trials, since jurors (at least theoretically) know nothing at all about the case before the trial, (or if they do, they are strictly instructed by the Judge to put ____13____ notions aside). Though such statements may be dramatic and vivid, they must be limited to the evidence reasonably expected to be presented during the ___14___. ___15___ generally conclude opening statements with a reminder that at the conclusion of evidence, the attorney will return to ask the fact-finder to find in his or her client's favor."(1)

11.	12.	13.	14.	15.
a. Those	a. confused	a. unbiased	a. month	a. public
b. All	b .confuzed	b. preconceived	b. week	b. Judge
c. An	c. constructed	c. unprejudiced	c. appeal	c. Plaintiff
d. As	d. instructed	d. unbiazed	d. trial	d. Attorneys

Passage 4

"Criminal law is the body of law that relates to ___16___. It proscribes conduct perceived as threatening, harmful, or otherwise endangering to the property, health, safety, and moral welfare of people inclusive of one's self. ___17___ criminal law is established by statute, which is to say that the laws are enacted by a ___18___. Criminal law includes the punishment and rehabilitation of people who ___19___ such laws. Criminal law varies according to jurisdiction, and differs from civil law, where emphasis is more on dispute resolution and victim compensation, rather than on punishment or rehabilitation. Criminal procedure is a formalized official activity that authenticates the fact of commission of a crime and authorizes punitive or rehabilitative treatment of the ___20___."(1)

NYS Court Officer-Trainee Exam Guide

16.	17.	18.	19.	20.
a. offense	a. No	a. politicians	a. honor	a. Judge
b. felony	b. Neither	b. legislature	b. obey	b. offender
c. violation	c. Most	c. politics	c. violate	c. attorney
d. crime	d. None	d. persons	d. adhere	d. plaintiff

Answers 1-20

1. b. barriers (Types of barriers (plural) are the subject of the passage.)
2. c. delay (The aim is to impede, decrease, lessen attacks.)
3. d. more (Again, the aim is to discourage attacks, not promote them.)
4. b. perimeter (Logic. Fences are usually at the boundary of properties.)
5. b. facilities (This is the correct spelling.)

6. c. a (Agrees with singular "practice".)
7. b. hundreds (Gramma. Agrees with 'of' fatalities)
8. c. managing (This is the correct spelling.)
9. d. crowd (Agrees with logic of the sentence.)
10. d. gatherings (logic of sentence and plural noun)

11. c. An (Correct grammar, agrees with singular noun "opening statement".)
12. c. constructed (Correct vocabulary meaning.)
13. b. preconceived (Vocabulary and logic of sentence.)
14. d. trial (Fits with logic of sentence.)
15. d. Attorneys (Reference to attorneys in the first sentence, and plural.)

16. d. crimes (Logic of paragraph and plural meaning.)
17. c. Most (Logic of passage.)
18. b. legislature (Logical meaning of sentence.)
19. c. violate (Logical meaning of sentence.)
20. b. offender (Logical meaning of passage.)

3. APPLYING FACTS AND INFORMATION TO GIVEN SITUATIONS

"This section of the written exam assesses your ability to take information which you have read and apply it to a specific situation defined by a given set of facts. Each question contains a brief paragraph which describes a regulation, procedure or law. The selection is followed by a description of a specific situation. Then a question is asked which requires you to apply the law, regulation, or procedure described in the paragraph to the specific situation. Remember that all of the information you need to answer the question is contained in the paragraph and in the description of the situation. You need to read and understand both before you attempt to answer the question."*

Question 1:

"Directions: Use the information preceding each question to answer the question. Only that information should be used in answering the questions. Do not use any prior knowledge you may have on the subject. Choose the alternative that best answers the question."*

Policy:
All subpoenaed records delivered to the criminal court in Bronx county must be stored in the Subpoenaed Records Section (Room 407). The Supervising Clerk of the section shall record the receipt of such records and index and file them according to the index number of the case. Subpoenaed records may not be viewed by any party without the presentation of a written order from the Judge assigned to the

case or the Judge presiding in the Special Term Part. The viewing of the records must be done in the presence of a Clerk or a Court Officer or Court Officer-Trainee, and such records may not be removed from the Subpoenaed Records room without a written judicial order.

Situation:

Court Officer-Trainee Beverly Patterson is filling-in for Larry Baker, the Supervising Clerk of the Subpoenaed Records Section who is in the Major's Office completing an incident report regarding missing subpoenaed records. Attorney Julian Gerritson approaches Court Officer-Trainee Patterson and presents a judicial order to view certain subpoenaed records. Gerritson is a former Court Officer who attended law school and is now in private practice. Gerritson asks permission from Court Officer-Trainee Patterson to take the records to the Part of the Judge who signed the order and where attorney Gerritson is on trial before him.

Based on the preceding policy and situation, which of the following statements is correct?

- A. Court Officer-Trainee Patterson should give permission to take the files to the courtroom as this will save time.
- B. Because Attorney Gerritson is a former Court Officer, he may take the files to the courtroom.
- C. Court Officer-Trainee Patterson should remind attorney Gerritson that he needs a specific court order allowing him to remove the files from the Subpoenaed Records room.
- D. Court Officer-Trainee Patterson should not allow attorney Gerritson to view the records because he does not have a proper order.

Answer:

C. Court Officer-Trainee Patterson should remind attorney Gerritson that he needs a written judicial order allowing him to remove the files from the Subpoenaed Records room.

Choice "A" is not correct because "...records may not be removed from the Subpoenaed Records room without a written judicial order." The attorney only had an order which allowed him to <u>view</u> the records. Choice "B" is not correct because the policy does not grant former employees any special privileges.
Choice "D" is not correct because the order does allow him to <u>view</u> the records. However, there is no authorization to take the records out of the Subpoenaed Records Room.

Question 2:

"Directions: Use the information preceding each question to answer the question. Only that information should be used in answering the questions. Do not use any prior knowledge you may have on the subject. Choose the alternative that best answers the question."*

Procedure:

Criminal Procedure Law 270.50: (CPL 270.50)
1. When the court is of the opinion that a viewing or observation by the jury of the premises or place where an offense on trial was allegedly committed...will be helpful to the jury in determining any material factual issue, it may in its discretion, at any time before the commencement of the summations, order that the jury be conducted

to such premises or place for such purpose in accordance with the provisions of this section.

2. In such case, the jury must be kept together throughout under the supervision of an appropriate public servant or servants appointed by the court, and the court itself must be present throughout. The prosecutor, the defendant and counsel for the defendant may as a matter of right be present throughout, but such right may be waived.

3. The purpose of such an inspection is solely to permit visual observation by the jury of the premises or place in question, and neither the court, the parties, counsel nor the jurors may engage in discussion or argumentation concerning the significance or implications of anything under observation or concerning any issue in the case.

Situation:

On September 17, 2019, Court Officer Sylvia Dawkins participates as per CPL 270.50 in a court ordered viewing of a place where an offense was allegedly committed.

Based on the preceding procedure and situation, which of the following statements is correct?

   A. Court Officer Dawkins is authorized to state her legal opinion to the jury because she is a Court Officer.
   B. If the defendant is not present, the viewing cannot proceed.
   C. For the viewing to proceed, the court must be present.
   D. During the viewing of the premises, jurors need not be kept together if it is lunchtime.

Answer:

C. For the viewing to proceed, the court must be present.

("...the court itself must be present throughout.")

Choice "A" is not correct because no conversation regarding the premises is allowed and also the procedure does not authorize a Court Officer to give opinion.

Choice "B" is not correct because the defendant has the option of waiving the right to attend. ("The prosecutor, the defendant and counsel for the defendant may as a matter of right be present throughout, but such right may be waived.")

Choice "D" is not correct because the procedure does not allow any exceptions for lunchtime.

Question 3:

"Directions: Use the information preceding each question to answer the question. Only that information should be used in answering the questions. Do not use any prior knowledge you may have on the subject. Choose the alternative that best answers the question."*

Procedure:

All persons entering the court building are subject to the following magnetometer procedure:

1. All members of the public, including adults and minors, must physically pass through the magnetometer scanning device.
2. All packages and other items must be scanned by the X-Ray unit.
3. Court employees with valid ID may enter by way of the "EA Gate" that bypasses the magnetometer stations.

4. All law enforcement officials with valid police officer or peace officer ID may also enter through the "EA Gate".
5. Attorneys with valid "A/C ID" may also enter through the "EA Gate".

Situation:

On Monday, August 19, 2019, at 9:30 a.m., Court Officer-Trainee Harold Benjamin is on duty at the first floor entrance magnetometers. Because the courtrooms and offices are very busy on Mondays, the lines at the magnetometer stations are very long. The first calendar calls in courtrooms are usually scheduled for 9:30 a.m. Although the Court Officers are processing the public as fast as possible, it is clear that many of the people on the magnetometer line might miss their calendar call.

Attorney Martin Osweld, who is well known to Court Officer-Trainee Harold Benjamin, approaches Court Officer-Trainee Benjamin. He is sweating profusely and says that he ran for three blocks so he wouldn't miss the calendar call at 9:30 a.m. Also, because he left his house in a hurry, he forgot his "A/C ID". He asks to be permitted to bypass the magnetometers.

Based on the preceding procedure and situation, which of the following statements is the best course of action for Court Officer-Trainee Benjamin to take?

  A. He should allow attorney Martin Osweld to bypass the magnetometer stations because he is an attorney.

  B. He should do a visual scan of the attorney to make sure there are no bulges on his clothes and then let him bypass the magnetometer stations.

C. He should inform the attorney that he is not authorized to let him bypass the magnetometer stations.

D. He should inform the attorney that he should borrow an "A/C ID" from another attorney so that he can bypass the magnetometer stations.

Answer:

C. He should inform the attorney that he is not authorized to let him bypass the magnetometer stations.

Choice "A" is not correct because attorneys must have an "A/C ID" to bypass the magnetometer stations.

Choice "B" is not correct because a "visual check" does not replace the requirement of possessing an "A/C ID".

Choice "D" is not correct because using another person's ID is logically never allowed and would negate the effectiveness of issuing "A/C ID" passes.

Question 4:

"Directions: Use the information preceding each question to answer the question. Only that information should be used in answering the questions. Do not use any prior knowledge you may have on the subject. Choose the alternative that best answers the question."*

Rule:

Family Court Act Section 205.4: Access to Family Court proceedings

(a) The Family Court is open to the public. Members of the public, including the news media, shall have access to all courtrooms, lobbies, public waiting areas and other common areas of Family Court otherwise open to individuals having business before the court.

(b) The general public or any person may be excluded from a courtroom only if the Judge presiding in the courtroom determines, on a case-by-case basis based upon supporting evidence, that such exclusion is warranted in that case....

c) When necessary to preserve the decorum of the proceedings, the Judge shall instruct representatives of the news media and others regarding the permissible use of the courtroom and other facilities of the court, the assignment of seats to representatives of the news media on an equitable basis, and any other matters that may affect the conduct of the proceedings and the well-being and safety of the litigants therein.

Situation:

Court Officer-Trainee Janet Goodwall is assigned to JD (Juvenile Delinquency) Part 16 in Family Court. At 10:00 a.m., defendant Eddie Davis, enters the courtroom and takes a seat, waiting for the 10:15 a.m. calendar call. A minute later, three young men also enter the courtroom. Court Officer-Trainee Goodwall recognizes the three as being members of a gang opposing the gang that the defendant is allegedly a member.

Based on the preceding rule and situation, which of the following statements is the best course of action for Court Officer-Trainee Benjamin to take?

   A. Inform the three young men that they must leave the courtroom.

   B. Make an announcement in the courtroom that there is developing a possibility of violence.

   C. Inform the Judge presiding so that he may consider the best action to take.

   D. Inform everyone that all court proceedings are adjourned to the following day.

Answer:

C. Inform the Judge presiding so that he may consider the best action to take.

(The rule makes it clear that the presence of members of the public in the courtroom is as "the Judge presiding in the courtroom determines". All the other choices involve the overreach of Court Officer authority, especially choice "D" which is a blatant example.)

NYS Court Officer-Trainee Exam Guide

4. CLERICAL CHECKING

"This section of the examination assesses your ability to determine whether different sets of words, numbers, names and codes are similar. No matter what the form of the item, you are required to scan the sets of information, identify where the sets differ, and use the directions to determine the correct answer."*

This type of question might at first glance seem easy. However, it is relatively tricky, especially if you are not a careful and deliberate reader. This is the type of question where the correct answer is right in front of you. All you have to do is to recognize it.

Consider the following example:

Directions: The following example consists of three sets of information. Compare the information in the three sets. On your answer sheet, mark:

Choice A: if none of the three sets are exactly alike
Choice B: if only the first and second sets are exactly alike
Choice C: if only the first and third sets are exactly alike
Choice D: if all the sets are exactly alike.

Set 1:

1973 Elks Dr. S.W.	1973 Elks Dr. S.W.	1973 Elks Dr. S.W.
1 (718) 972-7936	1 (718) 972-7936	1 (718) 972-7936
Maj. Jack Feinberg	Maj. Jack Feinberg	Maj. Jack Feinburg
File FCJD 38746/19	File FCJD 38746/19	File FCJD 38746/19

NYS Court Officer-Trainee Exam Guide

Suggestions:
1. Read the description of the answer choices carefully. It is very easy to mix-up the descriptions if you read too quickly or are nervous during the test.
2. If possible, try to keep your finger on the information line (or use a pencil, or sheet of paper under the line to help guide your eyes).
3. Do not read the lines as you would a novel. Compare a section of the information that is not too long or too short. For example, compare "1973 Elks" in the first column to "1973 Elks" in the second and third column, instead of trying to compare "1973 Elks Dr. S.W." all at once.

The answer in the above information set is:
Choice B: if only the first and second sets are exactly alike
The information in Column 3 is different from column 1 and 2 because "Maj. Jack Feinberg" in columns 1 and 2 is spelled "Maj. Jack Feinb<u>u</u>rg" in column 3 (a "<u>u</u>" instead of and "<u>e</u>" in Feinberg).

Set 1 Answer:

1973 Elks Dr. S.W.	1973 Elks Dr. S.W.	1973 Elks Dr. S.W.
1 (718) 972-7936	1 (718) 972-7936	1 (718) 972-7936
Maj. Jack Feinberg	Maj. Jack Feinberg	Maj. Jack **Feinburg**
File FCJD 38746/19	File FCJD 38746/19	File FCJD 38746/19

NYS Court Officer-Trainee Exam Guide

Now, consider set number 2:

Set 2:

CC Frank Elsconer	FCA 1012 (Abuse)	96738692-6728755
FCA 1012 (Abuse)	CC Frank Elsconer	FCA 1012 (Abuse)
96738692-6728755	783-482 Arthur Blvd.	783-482 Arthur Blvd.
783-482 Arthur Blvd.	96738692-6728755	CC Frank Elsconer

Choice A: if none of the three sets are exactly alike

Choice B: if only the first and second sets are exactly alike

Choice C: if only the first and third sets are exactly alike

Choice D: if all the sets are exactly alike.

The answer is:

Choice D: if all the sets are exactly alike.

(Even though the three sets of information are displayed on different lines, **the information in the sets is the same**. Remember, you are comparing the **information** in the three sets and NOT the order in which the information is presented.

Now, lets look at another example:

Set 3:

CC Frank Elsconer	**FCA 1012 (Abuse)**	96738692-6728755
FCA 1012 (Abuse)	CC Frank Elsconer	FCA 1012 (Abuse)
96738692-6728755	783-482 Arthur Blvd.	*783-482 Arthur Blvd.*
783-482 Arthur Blvd.	96738692-6728755	**CC Frank Elsconer**

Directions: The preceding example consists of three sets of information. Compare the information in the three sets. On your answer sheet, mark:

Choice A: if none of the three sets are exactly alike

Choice B: if only the first and second sets are exactly alike

Choice C: if only the first and third sets are exactly alike

Choice D: if all the sets are exactly alike.

The answer is:

Choice D: if all the sets are exactly alike.

(The **information** in set 3 is the same. Only the presentation (the different fonts) is different.)

Remember:
1. Different fonts do not change the information.
2. A different order of presentation of the information does not change the information.

For practice, compare the 5 sets of information on the following page.

NYS Court Officer-Trainee Exam Guide

Directions: The following example consists of five sets of information (1-5). Compare the information in the three sets, and on your answer sheet, mark:

Choice A: if none of the three sets are exactly alike
Choice B: if only the second and third sets are exactly alike
Choice C: if only the first and second sets are exactly alike
Choice D: if all the sets are exactly alike.

1. Magistrate J. Warner SCPA 1537, Sect. 2 File HKS-7398/2019 J. Eleanor K. Buller	1. Magistrate J. Warner SCPA 1537, Sect. 2 File HKS-7398/2019 J. Eleanor K. Buller	1. Magistrate J. Warner SCPA 1537, Sect. 2 File HKS-7938/2019 J. Eleanor K. Buller
2. HSP: 9/16/19 - E-Z 2854 East Endor St. Ct. Officer Villanoff Scranton, NY 11793	2. HSP: 9/16/19 - E-Z 2854 East Endor St. Ct. Officer Vilanoff Scranton, NY 11793	2. HSP: 9/16/19 - E-Z 2854 East Endor St. Ct. Officer Vilanoff Scranton, NY 11793
3. CPL 725 S. 725.18 Gregory Chan, JHO DAT 2754/2020 6/1 Van Allen - Ref. 854	3. CPL 725 S. 725.18 Gregory Chen, JHO DAT 2754/2020 6/1 Van Allen - Ref. 854	3. CPL 725 S. 725.18 Gregory Chan, JHO DAT 2754/2020 6/1 Van Allen - Ref. 845
4. Stanton & Fried, PC 871111765-364495 763- 985-2189 (PA) CPL 3030 - Amend.	4. Stanton & Fried, PC 871111765-364495 763- 985-2189 (PA) CPL 3030 - Amend.	4. Stanton & Fried, PC 871111765-364495 763- 985-2189 (PA) CPL 3080 - Amend.
5. Lorna P. Williams Magistrate J. Ruiz CO Frank Salvidore Hilary Harriet Stein	5. Lorna P. Williams Magistrate J. Ruiz CO Frank Savidore Hilary Harriet Stein	5. Lorna P. Williams Magistrate J. Ruiz CO Frank Savidore Hilary Harriet Stein

NYS Court Officer-Trainee Exam Guide

Answers (1-5)

Choice A: if none of the three sets are exactly alike
Choice B: if only the second and third sets are exactly alike
Choice C: if only the first and second sets are exactly alike
Choice D: if all the sets are exactly alike.

1. **Answer C** Magistrate J. Warner SCPA 1537, Sect. 2 File HKS-7398/2019 J. Eleanor K. Buller	1. Magistrate J. Warner SCPA 1537, Sect. 2 File HKS-7398/2019 J. Eleanor K. Buller	1. Magistrate J. Warner SCPA 1537, Sect. 2 File HKS-7**93**8/2019 J. Eleanor K. Buller
2. **Answer B** HSP: 9/16/19 - E-Z 2854 East Endor St. Ct. Officer V**illa**noff Scranton, NY 11793	2. HSP: 9/16/19 - E-Z 2854 East Endor St. Ct. Officer Vilanoff Scranton, NY 11793	2. HSP: 9/16/19 - E-Z 2854 East Endor St. Ct. Officer Vilanoff Scranton, NY 11793
3. **Answer A** CPL 725 S. 725.18 Gregory Chan, JHO DAT 2754/2020 6/1 Van Allen - Ref. 854	3. CPL 725 S. 725.18 Gregory Ch**en**, JHO DAT 2754/2020 6/1 Van Allen - Ref. 854	3. CPL 725 S. 725.18 Gregory Chan, JHO DAT 2754/2020 6/1 Van Allen - Ref. 8**45**
4. **Answer C** Stanton & Fried, PC 871111765-364495 763- 985-2189 (PA) CPL 3030 - Amend.	4. Stanton & Fried, PC 871111765-364495 763- 985-2189 (PA) CPL 3030 - Amend.	4. Stanton & Fried, PC 871111765-364495 763- 985-2189 (PA) CPL 3**080** - Amend.
5. **Answer B** Lorna P. Williams Magistrate J. Ruiz CO Frank S**alvid**ore Hilary Harriet Stein	5. Lorna P. Williams Magistrate J. Ruiz CO Frank Savidore Hilary Harriet Stein	5. Lorna P. Williams Magistrate J. Ruiz CO Frank Savidore Hilary Harriet Stein

NYS Court Officer-Trainee Exam Guide

Directions: The following example consists of five sets of information (6-10). Compare the information in the three sets, and on your answer sheet, mark:

Choice A: if none of the three sets are exactly alike
Choice B: if only the second and third sets are exactly alike
Choice C: if only the first and second sets are exactly alike
Choice D: if all the sets are exactly alike.

6. Judge Fred Buolton EPTL Amend. 39-19 License A9JG78M Davidson, Mark	6. Judge Fred Boulton EPTL Amend. 39-19 License A9JG78M Davidson, Mark	6. Judge Fred Boulton EPTL Amend. 39-19 License A9JG78M Davidson, Mark
7. Part 35J (1/29/2019) 1895 Beltway Ave. Section 6743-29835 Falls & Becker, PC	7. Part 35J (1/29/2019) 1895 Beltway Ave. Section 6743-29835 Falls & Becker, PC	7. Part 35J (1/29/2019) 1895 Beltway Ave. Section 6743-29385 Falls & Becker, PC
8. Druckner Blvd., East Files 68692-69735 3/9/2019, 4/27/19 COT Beverly Schein	8. Druckner Blvd., East Files 68692-69735 3/6/2019, 4/27/19 COT Beverly Schein	8. Druckner Blvd., East Files 68692-69735 3/9/2019, 4/27/19 GOT Beverly Schein
9. Parts 35J, 37B, 29A Referee J. Lamonter Putnam, Dutchess 867-386-2687 Ext. 7.	9. Parts 35J, 37B, 29A Referee J. Lamonter Putnam, Dutchess 867-386-2687 Ext. 7.	9. Parts 35J, 37B, 29A Referee J. Lamonter Putnam, Dutchess 867-386-2687 Ext. 7.
10. NYPD Section 395 Valerie Z. Acevedo Ref. Numb. 356964 FC File S-38568/19	10. NYPD Section 395 Valerie Z. Acevedo Ref. Numb. 326964 FC File S-38568/19	10. NYPD Section 395 Valerie Z. Acevedo Ref. Numb. 326964 FC File S-38568/19

Answers (6-10)

Choice A: if none of the three sets are exactly alike
Choice B: if only the second and third sets are exactly alike
Choice C: if only the first and second sets are exactly alike
Choice D: if all the sets are exactly alike.

6. **Answer B** Judge Fred B**uol**ton EPTL Amend. 39-19 License A9JG78M Davidson, Mark	6. Judge Fred Boulton EPTL Amend. 39-19 License A9JG78M Davidson, Mark	6. Judge Fred Boulton EPTL Amend. 39-19 License A9JG78M Davidson, Mark
7. **Answer C** Part 35J (1/29/2019) 1895 Beltway Ave. Section 6743-29835 Falls & Becker, PC	7. Part 35J (1/29/2019) 1895 Beltway Ave. Section 6743-29835 Falls & Becker, PC	7. Part 35J (1/29/2019) 1895 Beltway Ave. Section 6743-29**38**5 Falls & Becker, PC
8. **Answer A** Druckner Blvd., East Files 68692-69735 3/9/2019, 4/27/19 COT Beverly Schein	8. Druckner Blvd., East Files 68692-69735 3/**6**/2019, 4/27/19 COT Beverly Schein	8. Druckner Blvd., East Files 68692-69735 3/9/2019, 4/27/19 **GOT** Beverly Schein
9. **Answer D** Parts 35J, 37B, 29A Referee J. Lamonter Putnam, Dutchess 867-386-2687 Ext. 7.	9. Parts 35J, 37B, 29A Referee J. Lamonter Putnam, Dutchess 867-386-2687 Ext. 7.	9. Parts 35J, 37B, 29A Referee J. Lamonter Putnam, Dutchess 867-386-2687 Ext. 7.
10. **Answer B** NYPD Section 395 Valerie Z. Acevedo Ref. Numb. **356**964 FC File S-38568/19	10. NYPD Section 395 Valerie Z. Acevedo Ref. Numb. 326964 FC File S-38568/19	10. NYPD Section 395 Valerie Z. Acevedo Ref. Numb. 326964 FC File S-38568/19

Remember these 2 important points regarding different fonts and order of presentation of the information:

11. **2873 Batler Street** Samuel F. Hoterman 3672-2976 (2019) *Judge Peter D. West*	2873 Batler Street *Samuel F. Hoterman* 3672-2976 (2019) Judge Peter D. West	2873 Batler Street Samuel F. Hoterman **3672-2976 (2019)** Judge Peter D. West

Question:

Is the information in the above three sets the same or different?

Answer:

The information in the three sets is the SAME.

(Different fonts do not make the information different.)

---

12. 2873 Batler Street Samuel F. Hoterman 3672-2976 (2019) Judge Peter D. West	Samuel F. Hoterman Judge Peter D. West 3672-2976 (2019) 2873 Batler Street	Judge Peter D. West 3672-2976 (2019) 2873 Batler Street Samuel F. Hoterman

Question:

Is the information in the above three sets the same or different?

Answer:

The information in the three sets is the SAME.

(The fact that the information is presented on different lines does not make the information different. The information in the sets is the SAME.)

RECORD KEEPING

"These questions will assess your ability to read, combine and manipulate written information organized from several different sources."*

The above explanation is from the OCA sample written questions, 2014. The explanation precedes a simple example of the question. Here, we will first work with a simple example, and then continue to a more complicated and longer question in the practice exam.

"Directions: Answer the four questions based on the information contained in the following tables. Remember, all of the information needed to answer the questions correctly can be found in the tables. Complete the "Daily Breakdown of Cases" and "Summary of Cases" tables before you attempt to answer any of the questions."*

"Part" means Courtroom
"Date Filed" is date the first papers of the case were filed with the clerk of the court.
"Status" means the status of the case at the end of the court session.
"Money Award" means the amount of money that was awarded on that case. The money is usually awarded to the party seeking money damages and is paid by the party who was sued.

Table 1: Daily List of Cases Monday			
Part	Date Filed	Status of Case	Money Award
Part C	04/10/17	Dismissed	X
Part D	11/01/18	Settled	X
Part B	06/09/17	Adjourned	X
Part A	01/24/19	Settled	$12,400
Part D	03/12/18	Adjourned	X
Part C	05/07/17	Dismissed	X
Part D	05/13/18	Adjourned	X
Part A	07/24/19	Settled	$10,500

Note that "No Money award" could be indicated by an "X", or "0", or "---", or even the word "None", etc.

Table 2: Daily List of Cases Tuesday			
Part	Date Filed	Status of Case	Money Award
Part A	02/22/19	Defaulted	X
Part D	04/17/17	Settled	$11,275
Part A	11/13/17	Dismissed	X
Part B	06/22/18	Adjourned	X
Part D	10/28/19	Settled	$13,200
Part C	07/21/18	Adjourned	X
Part D	09/12/17	Settled	$14,000

Table 3: Daily Analysis of Cases: Monday and Tuesday			
Status of Case	Monday	Tuesday	Total Cases
Adjourned			
Defaulted			
Dismissed			
Settled - with Money Award			
Settled - with NO Money Award			
Total Cases			
Cases by Year Filed			
2017			
2018			
2019			
Total Cases			

Table 4: Summary of Cases from Monday and Tuesday					
Part	Case Status at End of Day			Settled With Money Award	Settled No Money Award	Total Cases
	Adjourned	Defaulted	Dismissed			
A						
B						
C						
D						

Note that tables 1 and 2 provide the information (the facts) about the cases that were in Parts (Courtrooms) A-D on Monday and Tuesday. The tables tell us what day the cases were first filed with the court and what happened to those cases in the Parts on Monday and Tuesday.

Courts are required to make periodic reports about cases they handle. Special summaries that organize and condense the information are prepared (example: the third and fourth tables). These last two tables are sometimes referred to as "summary tables" or "supplemental tables." Court Officers in different courts sometimes assist in the gathering of the information or in the preparation of the forms. Although Court Clerks are increasingly assuming these duties, it is important for Court Officers to understand these reports and also to know how to prepare Court Officer specific reports relating to other courtroom activity or unusual or aided incidents in the court building.

The two completed summary tables (tables 3 and 4) are on the next page:

Note: Most candidates use a check mark (✓) to indicate that they have posted information. They do this to prevent double-posting of an item (See pages 116-118 for examples.)
Also, most candidates use a "|" mark to indicate each posting to a supplementary table (See pages 119-120). They do this so that they will be able to easily count the total items posted in each cell of the table.

Completed summary tables

Table 3: Daily Analysis of Cases: Monday and Tuesday

Status of Case	Monday	Tuesday	Total Cases
Adjourned	3	2	5
Defaulted		1	1
Dismissed	2	1	3
Settled - with Money Award	2	3	5
Settled - with NO Money Award	1		1
Total Cases	8	7	15
Cases by Year Filed			
2017	3	3	6
2018	3	2	5
2019	2	2	4
Total Cases	8	7	15

Table 4: Summary of Cases from Monday and Tuesday

Part	Case Status at End of Day			Settled With Money Award	Settled No Money Award	Total Cases
	Adjourned	Defaulted	Dismissed			
A		1	1	2		4
B	2					2
C	1		2			3
D	2			3	1	6
	5	1	3	5	1	15**

** We added this row as a "double-check" to confirm that we accounted for all 15 cases.

Answer the following five questions based on the above tables:

(Note: although these five questions could be answered without filling-out the summary tables, on the exam the number of cases in each table is much greater (25-30). For speed and accuracy (on most questions), you will need to refer to the completed summary tables.)

1. What is the total number of cases that were settled-with money award and settled with no money award?
   A. 5
   B. 6
   C. 7
   D. 8

2. Which year had the greatest number of cases filed?
   A. 2016
   B. 2017
   C. 2018
   D. 2019

3. The total number of adjourned cases exceeds the total number of defaulted cases by:
   A. 6
   B. 5
   C. 4
   D. 3

4. The total number of cases dismissed plus the total number of cases defaulted is:
   A. 4
   B. 5
   C. 6
   D. 7

5. The Part that handled a total of four cases is part:
   A. Part A
   B. Part B
   C. Part C
   D. Part D

Answers

1. B. 6
2. B. 2017 (6 cases)
3. C. 4 (5 - 1 = 4)
4. A. 4 (3 + 1 = 4)
5. A. Part A

Sometimes, as part of a table question, you may be provided with a "coding" table such as this:

Part	Judge Presiding
A	Harrison
B	Ruiz
C	Vilatov
D	Chang

Question 5 (above) could be rephrased as follows:

5. The Judge that handled four cases is Judge:
   A. Harrison
   B. Ruiz
   C. Vilatov
   D. Chang

To answer this, you need to know the Part that handled four cases (Part A - and then refer to the above "coding" table to relate the Part letter to the Judge presiding in that Part - Judge Harrison.)

Answer:

5. A. Harrison

On the test they might also provide you with an information table that is not completely filled out, for example:

Daily List of Cases Tuesday			
Part	Date Filed	Status of Case	Money Award
Part A	02/22/19	Defaulted	X
Part D	04/17/17	Settled	$11,275
Part A	11/13/17	Dismissed	X
Part B	06/22/18	Adjourned	X
Part D	10/28/19	(????)	$13,200
Part C	07/21/18	Adjourned	X
Part D	09/12/17	Settled	$14,000

The preceding table has information (????) that needs to be filled-in.

The (????) is obviously "Settled" (because there is a money award). You would need to write-in "Settled" so that when you add the cases that were "Settled" you would include this case.

The much longer table question in the following practice exam will include a table question where you will need to:

1. Fill-in any missing information.
2. Use a "coding" table.
3. Complete the summary tables.
4. Answer 15 questions.

NYS Court Officer-Trainee Exam Guide

PRACTICE TEST QUESTIONS

(75 Questions: Time allowed: 3 hours)

Questions 1-15: Remembering Facts and Information

"Directions: Read the brief story below. Study it for five minutes. Then, turn the story over and wait for ten minutes before you answer the fifteen questions on the following page. Try to remember as many details of the incident without making any written notes."*

(At the end of the five minutes, the test monitor will collect this sheet and ten minutes after that, you will be instructed to begin the test by answering from memory the first fifteen questions relating to this story.)

On August 15, 2019, at 8:50 a.m., Court Officer-Trainee Donna Breighton was in the Court Officer locker room, getting ready to report to her Criminal Court Part 18C, when a message from the Captain came over her radio. Captain Charles Lamont stated that a fight had broken out in front of the court building, on Hamilton Avenue, and that all available officers were to rush to the scene. Because the locker room was located on the second floor of the ten-story building, Court Officer-Trainee Breighton and the three other officers that were in the locker room rushed down the stairs and within a couple of minutes were the first Court Officers to arrive at the scene.

A crowd of about twenty people had formed around the two men that were still fighting. They were both around twenty years old and wearing red T-shirts that revealed tattoos on their necks and shoulders. Court Officer-Trainee Breighton and the other three officers subdued the two individuals and asked for their IDs. One of them was named Evan Youngs and the other was named William Thompson. Upon further questioning, Evan Youngs stated that he was at the court building as a defendant in an auto theft case that was scheduled in Part 25A at 9:30 a.m. He also stated that the person with whom he was fighting was a member of his gang who had threatened his life if he implicated the gang in any way during his court proceeding. The other person, William Thompson, who had no ID on him, stated that he was at the court only to obtain a copy of his own court file and that Evan Youngs started the fight without any provocation.

A quick check by the Court Officer Administration Office revealed that a person named William Thompson had two outstanding arrest warrants. One warrant was a bench warrant for failure to appear in court for a scheduled court hearing and the other was a Family Court warrant for willful failure to pay child support. William Thompson stated that he was not aware that there were any arrest warrants filed against him. Based on all this, the Captain ordered that the two individuals be brought up to the Court Officer Administration Office on the seventh floor for further questioning.

At 9:27 a.m., the Captain thanked all the Court Officers involved and asked each of them to provide an incident report before 5:00 p.m. By 9:30 a.m., Court Officer-Trainee was in her Part, ready to start her court day.

Answer questions 1-15 based on the information provided in the passage which you have read.

NYS Court Officer-Trainee Exam Guide

1. The Criminal Court Part to which Court Officer-Trainee Donna Breighton is assigned is:
   A. Part 28A
   B. Part 18C
   C. Part 25A
   D. Part 18A

2. At what time did a message from the Captain come over Donna Breighton's radio stating that a fight had broken out in front of the court building?
   A. 9:50 a.m.
   B. 8:40 a.m.
   C. 9:10 a.m.
   D. 8:50 a.m.

3. The name of the Captain is:
   A. Captain Evan Youngs
   B. Captain Charles Thompson
   C. Captain John Hamilton
   D. Captain Charles Lamont

4. The locker room is located on the ___ floor.
   A. third
   B. second
   C. tenth
   D. seventh

5. How many other officers were in the locker room with Court Officer-Trainee Breighton?
   A. five
   B. four
   C. three
   D. two

6. About how many people were in the crowd that had formed around the two men that were fighting?
   A. twenty
   B. twenty-two
   C. thirty
   D. thirty-two

7. What color T-shirts were the two men wearing?
   A. blue
   B. red
   C. brown
   D. white

8. The name of the person who stated that he was at the court building as a defendant in an auto theft case was:
   A. Evan Youngs
   B. William Thompson
   C. Evan Thompson
   D. William Youngs

9. The person who did not have ID was:
   A. Evan Youngs
   B. William Thompson
   C. Evan Thompson
   D. William Youngs

10. How many outstanding warrants did one of the persons allegedly have?
    A. on
    B. two
    C. three
    D. four

11. At what time did the Captain thank all the Court Officers involved in the incident?
    A. 9:30 a.m.
    B. 8:50 a.m.
    C. 9:27 a.m.
    D. 9:35 a.m

12. One of the outstanding warrants of arrest was for:
    A. failure to pay spousal support
    B. failure to pay child support
    C. failure to pay court imposed bail
    D. failure to report residence address

13. What did the Captain ask the Court Officers to file before 5:00 p.m.?

A. time reports
B. incident reports
C. incidental reports
D. none of the above

14. The front of the building was on:

A. Jefferson Avenue
B. Washington Avenue
C. Hamilton Avenue
D. Johnson Avenue

15. Each of the two individuals involved in the fight was around ___ years old.

A. twenty
B. twenty-two
C. thirty
D. thirty-two

Questions 16-35: Reading, Understanding and Interpreting Written Material

"Directions: The three passages below each contain five numbered blanks. Below each passage are listed five sets of words numbered to match the blanks. Pick the word from each set which seems to make the most sense both in the sentence and the total paragraph."*

Passage 1

"Jury trials are used in a significant share of ___16___ criminal cases in almost all common law lawful systems (Singapore, for example, is ___17___ exception), and juries or lay judges have been incorporated into the legal systems of many civil law countries for criminal cases. Only the United States makes routine use of jury trials in a wide variety of non-criminal cases. Other common law legal jurisdictions use jury trials only in a very select class of cases that make up a ___18___ share of the overall civil docket (like malicious prosecution and false imprisonment suits in England and Wales), but true civil jury trials are almost entirely absent elsewhere in the ___19___. Some civil law jurisdictions, however, have arbitration panels where non-legally trained members decide cases in select subject-matter areas ___20___ to the arbitration panel members' areas of expertise."(1)

16.	17.	18.	19.	20.
a. miniscule	a. some	a. large	a. town	a. irelevant
b. serious	b. many	b. tiny	b. world	b. verelant
c. trappist	c. several	c. majority	c. village	c. relevant
d. previous	d. an	d. majority	d. street	d. revenant

Passage 2

"A vacation, or ___21___, is a leave of absence from a regular ___22___, or a specific trip or journey, usually for the purpose of recreation or tourism. People often take a vacation during specific holiday observances, or for specific festivals or celebrations. ___23___ are often spent with friends or family. A person may take a longer break from work, such as a sabbatical, gap year, or career break. The concept of taking a vacation is ___24___ recent invention, and has developed through the last ___25___ centuries. Historically, the idea of travel for recreation was a luxury that only wealthy people could afford. In the Puritan culture of early America, taking a break from work for reasons other than weekly observance of the Sabbath was frowned upon. However, the modern concept of

NYS Court Officer-Trainee Exam Guide

vacation was led by a later religious movement encouraging spiritual retreat and recreation. The notion of breaking from work periodically took root among the middle and working class."(1)

21.	22.	23.	24.	25.
a. workday	a. ocupation	a. Escape	a. some	a. one
b. nap	b. occupation	b. Vacations	b. several	b. two
c. labor	c. ocuppation	c. Repose	c. two	c. single
d. holiday	d. ocupattion	d. Travail	d. a	d. half

Passage 3

"The idea of a supreme court owes much to the framers of the United ___26___ constitution. It was while debating the division of powers between the legislative and executive ___27___ that delegates to the 1787 Constitutional Convention established the ___28___ for the national judiciary. Creating a "third branch" of government was a novel idea; in the English tradition, judicial matters had been treated as an aspect of royal (executive) authority. It was also proposed that the ___29___ should have a role in checking the executive power to exercise a veto or to revise laws. In the end the Framers of the Constitution compromised by sketching only a general outline of the judiciary, vesting of federal judicial power in "one supreme Court, and in such inferior Courts as the Congress may from time to time ordain and establish." They ___30___ neither the exact powers and prerogatives of the Supreme Court nor the organization of the Judicial Branch as a whole."(1)

26.	27.	28.	29.	30.
a. Emirates	a. department	a. perameters	a. dictary	a. falsified
b. States	b. division	b. parameters	b. villages	b. distorted
c. Kingdom	c. part	c. paremeters	c. judiciary	c. delineated
d. Ireland	d. departments	d. parrameters	d. cities	d. confused

Questions 31-35

"Directions: After reading the selection below, choose the answer for each question, based solely on what is stated in the passage."

CIVIL COURT OF THE CITY OF NEW YORK: Instructions for Filing a Small Claims(2)

JURISDICTION: The maximum claim in the Small Claims Part is $5,000.00. If you are a Claimant who lives OUTSIDE New York City, you must sue in the county where the Defendant either resides, has an office or a place of regular employment within New York City.

In Small Claims the claimant can be a private individual or a sole proprietor only. Use form CIV-SC-50. For each Small Claims action under $1,000, the fee is $15.00. For each Small Claims action between $1,000.01 and 5,000.00, the fee is $20.00. There is no additional postage fee for multiple Defendants.

Only one Claimant and one Defendant may be included on each form. If you are suing more than one Defendant, you must use a separate claim form for each Defendant. You must provide the full and correct NAME of the person or firm you are suing. You must provide the correct STREET ADDRESS of the person or firm you are suing. We cannot accept Post Office Box numbers for either the Claimant's address or the Defendant's address. Date and Sign the front of the form.

PAYMENT OF FEES: Fees can be paid by Bank Check, Tellers Check, Certified Check or attorney's check or by Money Order, made payable to "CLERK, CIVIL COURT." No personal or company checks will be accepted.

(2) Edited CIV-SC-66 (revised 9/06)

31. Which of the following four statements is not supported by the above paragraph?

A. A Post Office Box number cannot be accepted for the Claimant's address.

B. A Post Office Box number cannot be accepted for the Defendant's address.

C. The front of the form must be dated and signed.

D. Two defendant's may be included in each form.

32. The form to be used to start a small claims case is form:

A. Edited CIV-SC-66

B Edited CIV-SC-66 (revised 9/06)

C. CIV-SC-50

D. none of the above

33. Jack Herman wants to start three small claims cases. For one case, he wishes to file a claim for $895. The other two cases are for $4,900 each. What is the total amount of filing fee that he must pay?

A. $ 45.00

B. $ 50.00

C. $ 60.00

D.$ 55.00

34. Which of the following is not accepted to start a small claims case?

A. check

B. money order

C. Tellers Check

D. certified check

35. Which of the following statements is not supported by the above passage?

A. The form must be dated

B. The form must be signed.

C. A separate claim form must be used for each defendant.

D. Filing fees may be paid in cash.

NYS Court Officer-Trainee Exam Guide

Questions 36-45: Applying Facts and Information to Given Situations

"Directions: Use the information preceding each question to answer the question. Only that information should be used in answering the questions. Do not use any prior knowledge you may have on the subject. Choose the alternative that best answers the question."*

Question 36

Rule

Every Court Officer is issued and responsible for the proper maintenance and operation of a firearm. The firearm must be worn in a non-concealed holster while the Court Officer is on duty. While the Officer is not on duty, the Court Officer has the option of wearing it in a concealed holster. The firearm must be inspected yearly as per regulation FRI-38 and the Court Officer must file the verified inspection report within ten days of the inspection with the Office of Court Administration at 89 Willow Street. Failure to file the FRI-38 yearly report timely may result in a formal counseling and fine. Court Officers are also responsible for following any future rules that are issued regarding firearms.

Situation

Court Officer Lawrence Burstein has been issued a weapon. He wears it at work and is careful not to do anything contrary to firearms regulations. He often consults with fellow Court Officers to make sure that he is following correct procedure.

36. Which of the following statements by fellow Court Officers regarding firearms rules is not correct?

A. Even if Court Officer Burstein does not file his FRI-38, he might not be counseled or be compelled to pay a fine.

B. The firearm may be worn while off-duty.

C. It is mandatory that the firearm be inspected every year.

D. During the time that a Court Officer is on duty, the firearm must be worn in a concealed holster.

Questions 37-39

Rules

The following is a "Schedule of Civil Court Fees" provided to Court Officers to use when answering questions from the public.

Fee to place a case on the calendar for trial...................$ 125.00
Fee to file a motion...$ 45.00
Fee to file a jury demand...$ 65.00
Fee to file a stipulation of settlement............................$ 35.00
Fee to file a voluntary discontinuance...........................$ 35.00

Situation

Court Officer-Trainee Susan Hale is assigned to the second floor public area, near the main cashier office. The line of people waiting to file papers and pay fees is very long due to heavy volume. The Supervising Cashier asks Court Officer-Trainee Hale if she would help expedite the process of paying fees by helping the people on line prepare any amounts that they need for the services that they are requesting. Court Officer-Trainee Hale helps ten people with simple questions before she encounters a person on line who has several items she needs to file and pay for and who is uncertain as to whether she has enough cash to pay for all of them. The person needs to file one jury demand, two motions, three voluntary discontinuances, and must also place two cases on the calendar for trial.

37. Based on the preceding rule and situation, the best course of action for Court Officer-Trainee Hale to take is:

A. Advise the person that based on the large number of things she needs to file and pay for, it is advisable that she leave and return on a day when it is not as busy.

B. Tell the person that due to the large number of items that she must attend to, she should immediately speak with the Supervising Cashier so that she can be assisted first.

C. She should estimate the amount the person needs for fees.

D. She should escort the person to the front of the line so that her needs can be handled first.

38. Another person on line needs to place a case on the calendar and also needs to file two jury demands. The amount of money the person needs to pay is:

A. $ 180

B. $ 130

C. $ 245

D. $ 255

39. Another person on line works in a legal office. She was given a check for $200 to file six stipulations of settlement. She asks Court Officer-Trainee Hale if this is the correct amount. Based on the above

rules, what is the best response that Court Officer-Trainee Hale should give?

A. $ 200 is the correct amount.

B. The $ 200 is not the correct amount and therefore the person should return to the legal office where she works.

C. She should return to her legal office and rebuke the employee who gave her the check.

D. The correct amount is $ 210.

Question 40

Rule

The Criminal Court has a sign in every courtroom that reads "Cell phone use not permitted in courtroom." The sign in Part 25B is displayed prominently on a wall where it is visible for all the people in the courtroom to see.

Situation

Court Officer-Trainee Jeffrey Ward is assigned to Part 25B. During the court proceeding he notices an attorney who is a regular in the Part use his cell phone to contact someone.

40. Based on the above Rule and Situation, which of the following four choices is the best course of action for Court Officer-Trainee Ward to take?

A. Arrest the attorney because he is a regular in the Part and he should have known not to use his cell phone during court proceedings.

B. Don't say or do anything because taking action might disrupt the court proceeding.

C. Discreetly remind the attorney that cell phone use is not permitted and that if he continues to use his cell phone, you will take proper action.

D. Confiscate the cell phone and take it immediately to the Court Officer headquarters in the building.

NYS Court Officer-Trainee Exam Guide

Questions 41-60: Clerical Checking

Directions: The following example consists of five sets of information. Compare the information in the three sets, and on your answer sheet, mark:

Choice A: if none of the three sets are exactly alike
Choice B: if only the second and third sets are exactly alike
Choice C: if only the first and second sets are exactly alike
Choice D: if all the sets are exactly alike.

41. George Avenue W. Fonar Highway SW Judge Albert Wing WN 36784-2856HC	George Avenue W. Fonar Highway SW Judge Albert Wing WN 36784-2856HC	George Avenue W. Fonar Highway EW Judge Albert Wing WN 36784-2856HC
42. Folger, Hill, Samuel MHL 81.252 (a - k) 2287-37 Elton Ave. *Albany, Seneca E.*	Folger, Hill, Samuel MHL 81.25 (a - k) 2287-37 Elton Ave. Albany, Seneca E.	Folger, Hill, Samuel MHL 81.252 (a -_h) 2287-37 Elton Ave. Albany, Seneca E.
43. 753098-29833111 Parts 26C, 32A, 35D 6/17/19 and 7/12/19 16 Lark Ave. Albany	753098-298333111 Parts 26C, 32A, 35D 6/17/19 and 7/12/19 16 Lark Ave. Albany	753098-298333111 Parts 26C, 32A, 35D 6/17/19 and 7/12/19 16 Lark Ave. Albany
44. Maj. Al Benchkins AR: 749820, L9328 Witness Cora Gome S: 78392-26486457	Maj. Al Benchkins AR: 749820, L9328 Witness Cora Gome S: 78392-26486457	**Maj. Al Benchkins** AR: 749820, L9328 Witness Cora Gome S: 78392-26486457
45. Inc. Rep. J-387-2019 Clerk Vincent Tang Magistrate Domlers Peter Williams, Jr.	Inc. Rep. J-387-2019 Clerk Vincent Tang Magistrate Domlers Peter Williams, Jr.	Inc. Rep. J-387-2019 Clerk Vincent Tang Magistrate Domler Peter Williams, Jr.

NYS Court Officer-Trainee Exam Guide

Directions: The following example consists of five sets of information. Compare the information in the three sets, and on your answer sheet, mark:

Choice A: if all the sets are exactly alike.
Choice B: if only the second and third sets are exactly alike
Choice C: if only the first and second sets are exactly alike
Choice D: if none of the three sets are exactly alike

46. 989 Market Street Court Assistant Behr Rooms 7653, 4985 VTL 785-245:28672	989 Market Street Court Assistant Behr Rooms 7653, 4982 VTL 785-245:28675	989 Market Street Court Assistant Behr Rooms 7653, 4985 VTL 785-245:28675
47. Appointed 2/15/2017 JHO Sonya Bravado Vehicle: JR7845KF Floors 2, 7, 8 and 9	Appointed 2/15/2017 JHO Sonya Bravado **Vehicle: JR7845KF** Floors 2, 7, 8 and 9	Appointed 2/15/2017 JHO Sonya Bravado *Vehicle: JR7845KF* Floors 2, 7, 8 and 9
48. PL Section 265 (b) Judge S. Seymour Tracking 387654-28 Ref. Number 96-45E	PL Section 265 (b) Judge S. Seymour Tracking 387654-28 Ref. Number 96-45F	PL Section 265 (b) Judge S. Seymour Tracking 387654-28 Ref. Number 96-45F
49. Guardianship Rm. 9 Larchmont, Unger Archives 2017, 2018 Queens, NY 11365	Guardianship Rm. 9 **Larchmont, Unger** Archives 2017, 2018 Queens, NY 11365	Guardianship Rm. 6 Larchmont, Unger Archives 2017, 2018 Queens, NY 11365
50. 4876 Wyoming Ave. *Tricarinco, Muriel* Brooklyn and Bronx Violetta Harrison	4876 Wyoming Ave. Tricarinco, Muriel Brooklyn and Bronx Violetta Harrison	4876 Wyoming Ave. Tricarinco, Muriel Brooklyn and Bronx Violetta Harrisson

NYS Court Officer-Trainee Exam Guide

Directions: The following example consists of five sets of information. Compare the information in the three sets, and on your answer sheet, mark:

Choice A: if only the first and second sets are exactly alike
Choice B: if only the second and third sets are exactly alike
Choice C: if all the sets are exactly alike.
Choice D: if none of the three sets are exactly alike

51. Reports NF 116-789 3 Clerical Assistants Referee Porterman Frances Germanicus	Reports NF 116-189 3 Clerical Assistants Referee Porterman Frances Germanicus	Reports NF 116-189 3 Clerical Assistants Referee Porterman Frances Germanicus
52. Series H (387-392) Police Precinct 92 Interpreter Wanda S. Lieutenant Newburg	Series H (387-392) Police Precinct 92 Interpreter Wanda S. Lieutenant Newburg	Series H (387-392) Police Precint 92 Interpreter Wanda S. Lieutenant Newburg
53. 3785 Denver Blvd. SCPA 2876 & 3978 Brenkanowitz, Boris Diary 1/2/19 - 3/4/19	3785 Denver Blvd. SCPA 2876 & 3978 Brenkanowitz, Boris Diary 1/2/19 - 3/4/19	3785 Denver Blvd. SCPA 2876 & 3978 Brenkanowits, Boris Diary 1/2/19 - 3/4/19
54. Hassell, Silver, Kurt SSL 2978-49870 (b) FCA Codes A-Z Volunteer J. Richard	Hassell, Silver, Kurt SSL 2978-49870 (b) FCA Codes A-Z Volunteer J. Richard	Hassell, Silver, Kurt SSL 2978-49870 (d) FCA Codes A-Z Volunteer J. Richard
55. Washington Pkwy. 754-593 New Street Report 72569/2019 Janya H. Whiteman	Washington Pkwy. 754-539 New Street Report 72569/2019 Janya H. Whiteman	Washington Pkwy. 754-539 New Street Report 72569/2019 Janya H. Whiteman

NYS Court Officer-Trainee Exam Guide

Directions: The following example consists of five sets of information. Compare the information in the three sets, and on your answer sheet, mark:

Choice A: if only the second and third sets are exactly alike
Choice B: if only the first and second sets are exactly alike
Choice C: if all the sets are exactly alike.
Choice D: if none of the three sets are exactly alike

56. *Court Rep. Jones* 839-865 Seneca Hill Case Management Jay Street, Brooklyn	Court Rep. Jones 839-865 Seneca Hill Case Management Jay Street, Brooklyn	**Court Rep. Jones** 839-865 Seneca Hill Case Management Jay Street, Brooklyn
57. 759-28 Nancy Loop Guardianship Sect. 6 Tax Ref. Number 16 Chief Clerk Barlett	759-28 Nancy Loop Guardianship Sect. 9 Tax Ref. Number 16 Chief Clerk Barlet	759-28 Nancy Loop Guardianship Sect. 9 Tax Ref. Number 16 Chief Clerk Barlett
58. 28765/19, 38976/19 4920 Madison Ave. Family Offense Pt. 3 7659111187-3229	28765/19, 38976/19 4920 Madison Ave. Family Offense Pt. 3 76591111187-3229	28765/19, 38976/19 4920 Madison Ave. Family Offense Pt. 3 76591111187-3229
59. Tim Proctor (Albany) Tracking 676543298 Witness Neil Keller Accounting, Rm. 74	Tim Proctor (Albany) Tracking 676543298 Witness Neil Keller Accounting, Rm. 74	Tim Proctor (Albany) Tracking 67654398 Witness Neil Keller Accounting, Rm. 74
60. Supreme Criminal File CIV 1295/2019 Judge Tomas Grand Niagara & Columbia	Supreme Criminal File CIV 1295/2019 Judge Tomas Grant Niagara & Columbia	Supreme Criminal File CIV 1295/2019 Judge Tomas Grant Niagara & Columbia

Questions 61-75: Record Keeping

The following pages contain the following:
1. Three individual tables listing cases that appeared before Trial Judges in Criminal, Family, Civil Courts (Nov. 4, 2019 - November 8, 2019).
2. A coding table "Coding Table: Part / Judge Presiding".
3. Two summary tables to organize the information presented in the first three tables listing cases that appeared before Judges in Criminal, Family, Civil Courts (Nov. 4, 2019 - November 8, 2019)

Directions: Complete the two summary tables based on the information provided and then answer the fifteen questions that follow.
Note that only the answers to the fifteen questions will be graded and not the work done on the tables.

Criminal Court List of Cases On the Court Calendar Nov. 4, 2019 - November 8, 2019			
Judge Presiding	Date Case Filed	Case Disposition	Fine Imposed
Volter	4/27/18	Trial	X
Finnegan	3/12/17	Adjourned	
Finnegan	2/10/18	Trial	$1,000
Volter	6/16/18	Dismissed	
Finnegan	6/17/17	Trial	X
Volter	3/9/18	Defaulted	
Finnegan	2/1/17	Trial	$1,250
Volter	1/22/19	Adjourned	
Finnegan	6/7/19	Trial	X
Finnegan	3/29/19	Trial	X
Volter	2/6/19	Trial	$1,500
Finnegan	1/30/19	Adjourned	

Family Court
List of Cases On the Court Calendar
Nov. 4, 2019 - November 8, 2019

Judge Presiding	Date Case Filed	Case Disposition	Amount of Restitution Ordered
Ming	12/22/17	Trial	$750
Thomas	3/28/18	Adjourned	
Ming	11/15/18	Trial	X
Thomas	5/16/17	Dismissed	
Ming	3/6/18	Trial	$1,000
Ming	5/13/18	Adjourned	
Thomas	7/29/18	Defaulted	
Ming	2/17/19	Trial	$1,150
Ming	2/14/19	Adjourned	
Thomas	5/2/19	Dismissed	
Ming	3/6/19	Trial	X
Ming	4/21/19	Adjourned	

NYS Court Officer-Trainee Exam Guide

Civil Court List of Cases On the Court Calendar Nov. 4, 2019 - November 8, 2019			
Judge Presiding	Date Case Filed	Case Disposition	Settlement Award Amount
Hawkins	2/5/18	Adjourned	
Donato	6/19/17	Dismissed	
Donato	4/2/19	Adjourned	
Hawkins	7/21/17	Settled	X
Donato	10/29/18	Settled	$5,900
Hawkins	3/18/19	Adjourned	
Donato	9/15/18	Settled	$12,500
Donato	12/18/18	Adjourned	
Hawkins	2/4/19	Settled	X
Donato	2/15/19	Adjourned	
Hawkins	5/1/19	Defaulted	

Coding Table Part / Judge Presiding	
Part	Judge Presiding
CR9	Finnegan
CR12	Volter
FC3	Thomas
FC7	Ming
CIV24	Hawkins
CIV32	Donato

Summary Table 1:

Case Status	Cases on Calendar Nov. 4, 2019 - November 8, 2019			
	Criminal	Family	Civil	Total Cases
Adjourned				
Defaulted				
Dismissed				
Settled - with Money Award				
Settled - no money award				
Trial with Fine Imposed				
Trial with no fine imposed				
Trial with Restitution Ordered				
Trial with no Restitution Ordered				
Total Cases				
Cases by Date Filed				
2017				
2018				
2019				
Total Cases				

Summary Table 2:

| | Case Status at End of Day | | | Settled Money Award | Trial with Fine Imposed | Trial with Restitution Ordered |
Part Code	Adjourned	Defaulted	Dismissed			
CIV32						
CIV24						
FC7						
FC3						
CR12						
CR9						

(Note that in the above table only certain case status' are included.)

Questions 61-75

61. The total number of Adjourned case for the three courts is:

   A. 6
   B. 8
   C. 10
   D. 12

62. What is the total number of cases for the three courts?
   A. 30
   B. 35
   C. 36
   D. 34

63. The Judge who has code FC3 is Judge_____.
   A. Ming
   B. Thomas
   C. Finnegan
   D. Hawkins

64. The number of Adjourned Cases for all three courts exceeded the total number of Dismissed Cases for all three courts by ____.
   A. 6
   B. 7
   C. 8
   D. 10

65. The greatest total number of cases filed in all three courts in one year is:
   A. 7
   B. 15
   C. 35
   D. 13

66. The Judge that had the greatest number of dismissed cases is Judge_____.
   A. Donato
   B. Volter
   C. Thomas
   D. Ming

67. The number of cases that were "Settled With Money Award" is ____.
   A. 1
   B. 2
   C. 3
   D. 4

68. The two Judges that tied for the greatest number of adjourned cases are Judges _____ and Judge _____.
   A. Donato and Hawkins
   B. Hawkins and Ming
   C. Ming and Finnegan
   D. Donato and Ming

69. The total number of cases filed in 2017 plus 2019 is ____.
   A. 20
   B. 21
   C. 22
   D. 24

70. How many cases had the disposition "Trial With No Fine Imposed"?

    A. 4
    B. 3
    C. 2
    D. 1

71. How many Family Court cases were filed in 2018?

    A. 1
    B. 3
    C. 5
    D. 7

72. What is the total of Criminal Court adjourned cases plus Family Court dismissed cases?

    A. 2
    B. 5
    C. 3
    D. 4

73. What is the total number of cases disposed by "Trial WIth Fine Imposed" by Judges Volter and Finnegan?

    A. 2
    B. 5
    C. 3
    D. 4

74. The total number of dismissed cases in all three courts exceeds the total number of defaulted cases by _____.
   A. 1
   B. 2
   C. 3
   D. 7

75. Which three Judges did not have any "Defaulted" cases?
   A. Hawkins, Ming and Finnegan
   B. Donato, Thomas and Ming
   C. Ming, Volter and Hawkins
   D. Donato, Ming and Finnegan

End of Practice Test

NYS Court Officer-Trainee Exam Guide

PRACTICE TEST ANSWERS

(75 Questions: Time allowed: 3 hours)

Questions 1-15: Remembering Facts and Information
"Directions: Read the brief story below. Study it for five minutes. Then, turn the story over and wait for ten minutes before you answer the fifteen questions on the following page. Try to remember as many details of the incident without making any written notes."*

(At the end of the five minutes, the test monitor will collect this sheet and ten minutes after that, you will be instructed to begin the test by answering from memory the first fifteen questions relating to this story.)

On August 15, 2019, at 8:50 a.m., Court Officer-Trainee Donna Breighton was in the Court Officer locker room, getting ready to report to her Criminal Court Part 18C, when a message from the Captain came over her radio. Captain Charles Lamont stated that a fight had broken out in front of the court building, on Hamilton Avenue, and that all available officers were to rush to the scene. Because the locker room was located on the second floor of the ten-story building, Court Officer-Trainee Breighton and the three other officers that were in the locker room rushed down the stairs and within a couple of minutes were the first Court Officers to arrive at the scene.

A crowd of about twenty people had formed around the two men that were still fighting. They were both around twenty years old and wearing red T-shirts that revealed tattoos on their necks and shoulders. Court Officer-Trainee Breighton and the other three officers subdued the two individuals and asked for their IDs. One of them was named Evan Youngs and the other was named William Thompson. Upon further questioning, Evan Youngs stated that he was at the court building as a defendant in an auto theft case that was scheduled in Part 25A at 9:30 a.m. He also stated that the person with whom he was fighting was a member of his gang who had threatened his life if he implicated the gang in any way during his court proceeding. The other person, William Thompson, who had no ID on him, stated that he was at the court only to obtain a copy of his own court file and that Evan Youngs started the fight without any provocation.

A quick check by the Court Officer Administration Office revealed that a person named William Thompson had two outstanding arrest warrants. One warrant was a bench warrant for failure to appear in court for a scheduled court hearing and the other was a Family Court warrant for willful failure to pay child support. William Thompson stated that he was not aware that there were any arrest warrants filed against him. Based on all this, the Captain ordered that the two individuals be brought up to the Court Officer Administration Office on the seventh floor for further questioning.

At 9:27 a.m., the Captain thanked all the Court Officers involved and asked each of them to provide an incident report before 5:00 p.m. By 9:30 a.m., Court Officer-Trainee was in her Part, ready to start her court day.

Answer questions 1-15 based on the information provided in the passage which you have read.

1. The Criminal Court Part to which Court Officer-Trainee Donna Breighton is assigned is:
   A. Part 28A
   B. Part 18C
   C. Part 25A
   D. Part 18A

2. At what time did a message from the Captain come over Donna Breighton's radio stating that a fight had broken out in front of the court building?
   A. 9:50 a.m.
   B. 8:40 a.m.
   C. 9:10 a.m.
   D. 8:50 a.m.

3. The name of the Captain is:
   A. Captain Evan Youngs
   B. Captain Charles Thompson
   C. Captain John Hamilton
   D. Captain Charles Lamont

4. The locker room is located on the ___ floor.
   A. third
   B. second
   C. tenth
   D. seventh

5. How many other officers were in the locker room with Court Officer-Trainee Breighton?

   A. five

   C. three

   B. four

   D. two

6. About how many people were in the crowd that had formed around the two men that were fighting?

   A. twenty

   C. thirty

   B. twenty-two

   D. thirty-two

7. What color T-shirts were the two men wearing?

   A. blue

   C. brown

   B. red

   D. white

8. The name of the person who stated that he was at the court building as a defendant in an auto theft case was:

   A. Evan Youngs

   C. Evan Thompson

   B. William Thompson

   D. William Youngs

9. The person who did not have ID was:

   A. Evan Youngs

   C. Evan Thompson

   B. William Thompson

   D. William Youngs

10. How many outstanding warrants did one of the persons allegedly have?

    A. on

    C. three

    B. two

    D. four

11. At what time did the Captain thank all the Court Officers involved in the incident?
    A. 9:30 a.m.
    C. 9:27 a.m.
    B. 8:50 a.m.
    D. 9:35 a.m.

12. One of the outstanding warrants of arrest was for:
    A. failure to pay spousal support
    B. failure to pay child support
    C. failure to pay court imposed bail
    D. failure to report residence address

13. What did the Captain ask the Court Officers to file before 5:00 p.m.?
    A. time reports
    C. incidental reports
    B. incident reports
    D. none of the above

14. The front of the building was on:
    A. Jefferson Avenue
    C. Hamilton Avenue
    B. Washington Avenue
    D. Johnson Avenue

15. Each of the two individuals involved in the fight was around ___ years old.
    A. twenty
    C. thirty
    B. twenty-two
    D. thirty-two

NYS Court Officer-Trainee Exam Guide

Questions 16-35: Reading, Understanding and Interpreting Written Material

"Directions: The three passages below each contain five numbered blanks. Below each passage are listed five sets of words numbered to match the blanks. Pick the word from each set which seems to make the most sense both in the sentence and the total paragraph."*

Passage 1

"Jury trials are used in a significant share of ____16____ criminal cases in almost all common law lawful systems (Singapore, for example, is ____17____ exception), and juries or lay judges have been incorporated into the legal systems of many civil law countries for criminal cases. Only the United States makes routine use of jury trials in a wide variety of non-criminal cases. Other common law legal jurisdictions use jury trials only in a very select class of cases that make up a ____18____ share of the overall civil docket (like malicious prosecution and false imprisonment suits in England and Wales), but true civil jury trials are almost entirely absent elsewhere in the ____19____. Some civil law jurisdictions, however, have arbitration panels where non-legally trained members decide cases in select subject-matter areas ____20____ to the arbitration panel members' areas of expertise."(1)

16.	17.	18.	19.	20.
a. miniscule	a. some	a. large	a. town	a. irelevant
b. serious	b. many	**b. tiny**	**b. world**	b. verelant
c. trappist	c. several	c. majority	c. village	**c. relevant**
d. previous	**d. an**	d. majority	d. street	d. revenant

NYS Court Officer-Trainee Exam Guide

Answers

16. b. serious (logical meaning)

17. d. an (grammar, singular)

18. b. tiny (logic: "select" number of cases)

19. b. world (logic)

20. c. relevant (spelling and vocabulary meaning)

Passage 2

"A vacation, or ____21____, is a leave of absence from a regular ____22____, or a specific trip or journey, usually for the purpose of recreation or tourism. People often take a vacation during specific holiday observances, or for specific festivals or celebrations. ____23____ are often spent with friends or family. A person may take a longer break from work, such as a sabbatical, gap year, or career break. The concept of taking a vacation is ____24____ recent invention, and has developed through the last ____25____ centuries. Historically, the idea of travel for recreation was a luxury that only wealthy people could afford. In the Puritan culture of early America, taking a break from work for reasons other than weekly observance of the Sabbath was frowned upon. However, the modern concept of vacation was led by a later religious movement encouraging spiritual retreat and recreation. The notion of breaking from work periodically took root among the middle and working class."(1)

21.	22.	23.	24.	25.
a. workday	a. ocupation	a. Escape	a. some	a. one
b. nap	**b. occupation**	**b. Vacations**	b. several	**b. two**
c. labor	c. ocuppation	c. Repose	c. two	c. single
d. holiday	d. ocupattion	d. Travail	**d. a**	d. half

Answers

21. d. holiday (meaning, logic, synonym for vacation)

22. b. occupation (spelling)

23. b. Vacations (vocabulary and logical agreement with passage)

24. d. a (grammar: singular)

25. b. two (grammar: plural)

Passage 3

"The idea of a supreme court owes much to the framers of the United ___26___ constitution. It was while debating the division of powers between the legislative and executive ___27___ that delegates to the 1787 Constitutional Convention established the ___28___ for the national judiciary. Creating a "third branch" of government was a novel idea; in the English tradition, judicial matters had been treated as an aspect of royal (executive) authority. It was also proposed that the ___29___ should have a role in checking the executive power to exercise a veto or to revise laws. In the end the Framers of the Constitution compromised by sketching only a general outline of the judiciary, vesting of federal judicial power in "one supreme Court, and in such inferior Courts as the Congress may from time to time ordain and establish." They ___30___ neither the exact powers and prerogatives of the Supreme Court nor the organization of the Judicial Branch as a whole."(1)

26.	27.	28.	29.	30.
a. Emirates	a. department	a. perameters	a. dictary	a. falsified
b. States	b. division	**b. parameters**	b. villages	b. distorted
c. Kingdom	c. part	c. paremeters	**c. judiciary**	**c. delineated**
d. Ireland	**d. departments**	d. parrameters	d. cities	d. confused

Answers

26. b. States (to agree with "1787 Constitutional Convention")

27. d. departments (grammar: plural)

28. b. parameters (spelling)

29. c. judiciary (logic)

30. c. delineated (vocabulary)

Questions 31-35

"Directions: After reading the selection below, choose the answer for each question, based solely on what is stated in the passage."

CIVIL COURT OF THE CITY OF NEW YORK: Instructions for Filing a Small Claims(2)

JURISDICTION: The maximum claim in the Small Claims Part is $5,000.00. If you are a Claimant who lives OUTSIDE New York City, you must sue in the county where the Defendant either resides, has an office or a place of regular employment within New York City.

In Small Claims the claimant can be a private individual or a sole proprietor only. Use form CIV-SC-50. For each Small Claims action under $1,000, the fee is $15.00. For each Small Claims action between $1,000.01 and 5,000.00, the fee is $20.00. There is no additional postage fee for multiple Defendants.

Only one Claimant and one Defendant may be included on each form. If you are suing more than one Defendant, you must use a separate claim form for each Defendant. You must provide the full and correct NAME of the person or firm you are suing. You must provide the correct STREET ADDRESS of the person or firm you are suing. We cannot accept Post Office Box numbers for either the Claimant's address or the Defendant's address. Date and Sign the front of the form.

PAYMENT OF FEES: Fees can be paid by Bank Check, Tellers Check, Certified Check or attorney's check or by Money Order, made payable to "CLERK, CIVIL COURT." No personal or company checks will be accepted.

(2) Edited CIV-SC-66 (revised 9/06)

31. Which of the following four statements is not supported by the above paragraph?

A. A Post Office Box number cannot be accepted for the Claimant's address.

B. A Post Office Box number cannot be accepted for the Defendant's address.

C. The front of the form must be dated and signed.

D. Two defendant's may be included in each form.

32. The form to be used to start a small claims case is form:

A. Edited CIV-SC-66

B Edited CIV-SC-66 (revised 9/06)

C. CIV-SC-50

D. none of the above

33. Jack Herman wants to start three small claims cases. For one case, he wishes to file a claim for $895. The other two cases are for $4,900 each. What is the total amount of filing fee that he must pay?

A. $ 45.00

B. $ 50.00

C. $ 60.00

D.$ 55.00 ($15.00 + $20.00 + $20.00 = $55.00)

34. Which of the following is not accepted to start a small claims case?

A. check

B. money order

C. Tellers Check

D. certified check

35. Which of the following statements is not supported by the above passage?

A. The form must be dated

B. The form must be signed.

C. A separate claim form must be used for each defendant.

D. Filing fees may be paid in cash.

NYS Court Officer-Trainee Exam Guide

Questions 36-45: Applying Facts and Information to Given Situations

"Directions: Use the information preceding each question to answer the question. Only that information should be used in answering the questions. Do not use any prior knowledge you may have on the subject. Choose the alternative that best answers the question."*

Question 36

Rule

Every Court Officer is issued and responsible for the proper maintenance and operation of a firearm. The firearm must be worn in a non-concealed holster while the Court Officer is on duty. While the Officer is not on duty, the Court Officer has the option of wearing it in a concealed holster. The firearm must be inspected yearly as per regulation FRI-38 and the Court Officer must file the verified inspection report within ten days of the inspection with the Office of Court Administration at 89 Willow Street. Failure to file the FRI-38 yearly report timely may result in a formal counseling and fine. Court Officers are also responsible for following any future rules that are issued regarding firearms.

Situation

Court Officer Lawrence Burstein has been issued a weapon. He wears it at work and is careful not to do anything contrary to firearms regulations. He often consults with fellow Court Officers to make sure that he is following correct procedure.

36. Which of the following statements by fellow Court Officers regarding firearms rules is not correct?

A. Even if Court Officer Burstein does not file his FRI-38, he might not be counseled or be compelled to pay a fine.

B. The firearm may be worn while off-duty.

C. It is mandatory that the firearm be inspected every year.

D. During the time that a Court Officer is on duty, the firearm must be worn in a concealed holster.

(Choice D is the answer because "The firearm must be worn in a **non-concealed** holster while the Court Officer is on duty.")

Questions 37-39

Rules

The following is a "Schedule of Civil Court Fees" provided to Court Officers to use when answering questions from the public.

Fee to place a case on the calendar for trial...................$ 125.00
Fee to file a motion...$ 45.00
Fee to file a jury demand.. $ 65.00
Fee to file a stipulation of settlement............................. $ 35.00
Fee to file a voluntary discontinuance...........................$ 35.00

Situation

Court Officer-Trainee Susan Hale is assigned to the second floor public area, near the main cashier office. The line of people waiting to file papers and pay fees is very long due to heavy volume. The Supervising Cashier asks Court Officer-Trainee Hale if she could help expedite the process of paying fees by helping the people on line prepare any amounts that they need for the services that they are requesting. Court Officer-Trainee Hale helps ten people with simple questions before she encounters a person on line who has several items she needs to file and pay for and who is uncertain as to whether she has enough cash to pay for all of them. The person needs to file one jury demand, two motions, three voluntary discontinuances, and must also place two cases on the calendar for trial.

37. Based on the preceding rule and situation, the best course of action for Court Officer-Trainee Hale to take is:

A. Advise the person that based on the large number of things she needs to file and pay for, it is advisable that she leave and return on a day when it is not as busy.

B. Tell the person that due to the large number of items that she must attend to, she should immediately speak with the Supervising Cashier so that she can be assisted first.

C. She should estimate the amount the person needs for fees.

D. She should escort the person to the front of the line so that her needs can be handled first.

The answer is C. Court Officer-Trainee Hale has enough information to estimate how much the person needs to pay. Taking the person out of line or asking the person to return would not be good quality service and would be defeating the reason why she was asked to answer questions - to speed up the line.

38. Another person on line needs to place a case on the calendar and also needs to file two jury demands. The amount of money the person needs to pay is:

A. $ 180

B. $ 130

C. $ 245

D. $ 255

Answer is: D. $255 ($125 to place a case on the calendar + 2 X 65 to file 2 jury demands = $255)

39. Another person on line works in a legal office. She was given a check for $200 to file six stipulations of settlement. She asks Court Officer-Trainee Hale if this is the correct amount. Based on the above rules, what is the best response that Court Officer-Trainee Hale should give?

A. $ 200 is the correct amount.

B. The $ 200 is not the correct amount and therefore the person should return to the legal office where she works.

C. She should return to her legal office and rebuke the employee who gave her the check.

D. The correct amount is $210.

The answer is D. By stating the correct amount, Court Officer-Trainee Hale is answering the question directly without anticipating what the person might decide to do about the situation, or what the person's next question might be.

Question 40

Rule

The Criminal Court has a sign in every courtroom that reads "Cell phone use not permitted in courtroom." The sign in Part 25B is displayed prominently on a wall where it is visible for all the people in the courtroom to see.

NYS Court Officer-Trainee Exam Guide

Situation

Court Officer-Trainee Jeffrey Ward is assigned to Part 25B. During the court proceeding he notices an attorney who is a regular in the Part use his cell phone to contact someone.

40. Based on the above Rule and Situation, which of the following four choices is the best course of action for Court Officer-Trainee Ward to take?

A. Arrest the attorney because he is a regular in the Part and he should have known not to use his cell phone during court proceedings.

B. Don't say or do anything because taking action might disrupt the court proceeding.

C. Discreetly remind the attorney that cell phone use is not permitted and that if he continues to use his cell phone, you will take proper action.

D. Confiscate the cell phone and take it immediately to the Court Officer headquarters in the building.

Answer is: C. Discreetly remind the attorney that cell phone use is not permitted and that if he continues to use his cell phone, you will take proper action.

Choices "A" and "D" are overreactions and therefore not the best actions. Choice "B" is not a good choice because the attorney was violating a policy against use of cell phones in the courtroom and at least a warning to the attorney is necessary.

NYS Court Officer-Trainee Exam Guide

Questions 41-60: Clerical Checking

Directions: The following example consists of five sets of information. Compare the information in the three sets, and on your answer sheet, mark:

Choice A: if none of the three sets are exactly alike
Choice B: if only the second and third sets are exactly alike
Choice C: if only the first and second sets are exactly alike
Choice D: if all the sets are exactly alike.

41. **Answer C** George Avenue W. Fonar Highway SW Judge Albert Wing WN 36784-2856HC	George Avenue W. Fonar Highway SW Judge Albert Wing WN 36784-2856HC	George Avenue W. Fonar Highway **EW** Judge Albert Wing WN 36784-2856HC
42. **Answer A** Folger, Hill, Samuel MHL 81.252 (a - k) 2287-37 Elton Ave. *Albany, Seneca E.*	Folger, Hill, Samuel MHL 81.**25** (a - k) 2287-37 Elton Ave. Albany, Seneca E.	Folger, Hill, Samuel MHL 81.252 (a - **h**) 2287-37† Elton Ave. Albany, Seneca E.
43. **Answer B** 753098-298**3311**1 Parts 26C, 32A, 35D 6/17/19 and 7/12/19 16 Lark Ave. Albany	753098-298333111 Parts 26C, 32A, 35D 6/17/19 and 7/12/19 16 Lark Ave. Albany	753098-298333111 Parts 26C, 32A, 35D 6/17/19 and 7/12/19 16 Lark Ave. Albany
44. **Answer D** Maj. Al Benchkins AR: 749820, L9328 Witness Cora Gome S: 78392-26486457	Maj. Al Benchkins AR: 749820, L9328 Witness Cora Gome S: 78392-26486457	**Maj. Al Benchkins** AR: 749820, L9328 Witness Cora Gome S: 78392-26486457
45. **Answer C** Inc. Rep. J-387-2019 Clerk Vincent Tang Magistrate Domlers Peter Williams, Jr.	Inc. Rep. J-387-2019 Clerk Vincent Tang Magistrate Domlers Peter Williams, Jr.	Inc. Rep. J-387-2019 Clerk Vincent Tang Magistrate Do**mler** Peter Williams, Jr.

NYS Court Officer-Trainee Exam Guide

Directions: The following example consists of five sets of information. Compare the information in the three sets, and on your answer sheet, mark:

Choice A: if all the sets are exactly alike.
Choice B: if only the second and third sets are exactly alike
Choice C: if only the first and second sets are exactly alike
Choice D: if none of the three sets are exactly alike

46. **Answer D** 989 Market Street Court Assistant Behr Rooms 7653, 4985 VTL 785-245:286**72**	989 Market Street Court Assistant Behr Rooms 7653, 49**82** VTL 785-245:28675	989 Market Street Court Assistant Behr Rooms 7653, 4985 VTL 785-245:28675
47. **Answer A** Appointed 2/15/2017 JHO Sonya Bravado Vehicle: JR7845KF Floors 2, 7, 8 and 9	Appointed 2/15/2017 JHO Sonya Bravado **Vehicle: JR7845KF** Floors 2, 7, 8 and 9	Appointed 2/15/2017 JHO Sonya Bravado *Vehicle: JR7845KF* Floors 2, 7, 8 and 9
48. **Answer B** PL Section 265 (b) Judge S. Seymour Tracking 387654-28 Ref. Number 96-4**5E**	PL Section 265 (b) Judge S. Seymour Tracking 387654-28 Ref. Number 96-45F	PL Section 265 (b) Judge S. Seymour Tracking 387654-28 Ref. Number 96-45F
49. **Answer C** Guardianship Rm. 9 Larchmont, Unger Archives 2017, 2018 Queens, NY 11365	Guardianship Rm. 9 **Larchmont, Unger** Archives 2017, 2018 Queens, NY 11365	Guardianship Rm. **6** Larchmont, Unger Archives 2017, 2018 Queens, NY 11365
50. **Answer C** 4876 Wyoming Ave. *Tricarinco, Muriel* Brooklyn and Bronx Violetta Harrison	4876 Wyoming Ave. Tricarinco, Muriel Brooklyn and Bronx Violetta Harrison	4876 Wyoming Ave. Tricarinco, Muriel Brooklyn and Bronx Violetta Harr**isso**n

NYS Court Officer-Trainee Exam Guide

Directions: The following example consists of five sets of information. Compare the information in the three sets, and on your answer sheet, mark:

Choice A: if only the first and second sets are exactly alike
Choice B: if only the second and third sets are exactly alike
Choice C: if all the sets are exactly alike.
Choice D: if none of the three sets are exactly alike

51. **Answer B** Reports NF 116-**789** 3 Clerical Assistants Referee Porterman Frances Germanicus	Reports NF 116-189 3 Clerical Assistants Referee Porterman Frances Germanicus	Reports NF 116-189 3 Clerical Assistants Referee Porterman Frances Germanicus
52. **Answer A** Series H (387-392) Police Precinct 92 Interpreter Wanda S. Lieutenant Newburg	Series H (387-392) Police Precinct 92 Interpreter Wanda S. Lieutenant Newburg	Series H (387-392) Police Pre**cint** 92 Interpreter Wanda S. Lieutenant Newburg
53. **Answer A** 3785 Denver Blvd. SCPA 2876 & 3978 Brenkanowitz, Boris Diary 1/2/19 - 3/4/19	3785 Denver Blvd. SCPA 2876 & 3978 Brenkanowitz, Boris Diary 1/2/19 - 3/4/19	3785 Denver Blvd. SCPA 2876 & 3978 Brenkano**wits**, Boris Diary 1/2/19 - 3/4/19
54. **Answer A** Hassell, Silver, Kurt SSL 2978-49870 (b) FCA Codes A-Z Volunteer J. Richard	Hassell, Silver, Kurt SSL 2978-49870 (b) FCA Codes A-Z Volunteer J. Richard	Hassell, Silver, Kurt SSL 2978-49870 **(d)** FCA Codes A-Z Volunteer J. Richard
55. **Answer B** Washington Pkwy. 754-**593** New Street Report 72569/2019 Janya H. Whiteman	Washington Pkwy. 754-539 New Street Report 72569/2019 Janya H. Whiteman	Washington Pkwy. 754-539 New Street Report 72569/2019 Janya H. Whiteman

NYS Court Officer-Trainee Exam Guide

Directions: The following example consists of five sets of information. Compare the information in the three sets, and on your answer sheet, mark:

Choice A: if only the second and third sets are exactly alike
Choice B: if only the first and second sets are exactly alike
Choice C: if all the sets are exactly alike.
Choice D: if none of the three sets are exactly alike

56. **Answer C** *Court Rep. Jones* 839-865 Seneca Hill Case Management Jay Street, Brooklyn	Court Rep. Jones 839-865 Seneca Hill Case Management Jay Street, Brooklyn	**Court Rep. Jones** 839-865 Seneca Hill Case Management Jay Street, Brooklyn
57. **Answer D** 759-28 Nancy Loop Guardianship Sect. **6** Tax Ref. Number 16 Chief Clerk Barlett	759-28 Nancy Loop Guardianship Sect. 9 Tax Ref. Number 16 Chief Clerk Ba**rlet**	759-28 Nancy Loop Guardianship Sect. 9 Tax Ref. Number 16 Chief Clerk Barlett
58. **Answer A** 28765/19, 38976/19 4920 Madison Ave. Family Offense Pt. 3 7659**111187**-3229	28765/19, 38976/19 4920 Madison Ave. Family Offense Pt. 3 76591111187-3229	28765/19, 38976/19 4920 Madison Ave. Family Offense Pt. 3 76591111187-3229
59. **Answer B** Tim Proctor (Albany) Tracking 676543298 Witness Neil Keller Accounting, Rm. 74	Tim Proctor (Albany) Tracking 676543298 Witness Neil Keller Accounting, Rm. 74	Tim Proctor (Albany) Tracking 67654**439**8 Witness Neil Keller Accounting, Rm. 74
60. **Answer A** Supreme Criminal File CIV 1295/2019 Judge Tomas Gra**nd** Niagara & Columbia	Supreme Criminal File CIV 1295/2019 Judge Tomas Grant Niagara & Columbia	Supreme Criminal File CIV 1295/2019 Judge Tomas Grant Niagara & Columbia

Questions 61-75: Record Keeping

The following pages contain the following:
1. Three individual tables listing cases that appeared before Trial Judges in Criminal, Family, Civil Courts (Nov. 4, 2019 - November 8, 2019).
2. A coding table "Coding Table: Part / Judge Presiding".
3. Two summary tables to organize the information presented in the first three tables listing cases that appeared before Judges in Criminal, Family, Civil Courts (Nov. 4, 2019 - November 8, 2019)

Directions: Complete the two summary tables based on the information provided and then answer the fifteen questions that follow.
Note that only the answers to the fifteen questions will be graded and not the work done on the tables.

\multicolumn{4}{c	}{Criminal Court List of Cases On the Court Calendar Nov. 4, 2019 - November 8, 2019}
Judge Presiding	Date Case Filed	Case Disposition	Fine Imposed
Volter *CR12*	4/27/18 ✓	Trial ✓ ✓	X
Finnegan *CR9*	3/12/17 ✓	Adjourned ✓ ✓	
Finnegan *CR9*	2/10/18 ✓	Trial ✓ ✓	$1,000
Volter *CR12*	6/16/18 ✓	Dismissed ✓ ✓	
Finnegan *CR9*	6/17/17 ✓	Trial ✓ ✓	X
Volter *CR12*	3/9/18 ✓	Defaulted ✓ ✓	
Finnegan *CR9*	2/1/17 ✓	Trial ✓ ✓	$1,250
Volter *CR12*	1/22/19 ✓	Adjourned ✓ ✓	
Finnegan *CR9*	6/7/19 ✓	Trial ✓ ✓	X
Finnegan *CR9*	3/29/19 ✓	Trial ✓ ✓	X
Volter *CR12*	2/6/19 ✓	Trial ✓ ✓	$1,500
Finnegan *CR9*	1/30/19 ✓	Adjourned ✓ ✓	

Family Court List of Cases On the Court Calendar Nov. 4, 2019 - November 8, 2019			
Judge Presiding	Date Case Filed	Case Disposition	Amount of Restitution Ordered
Ming FC7	12/22/17 ✓	Trial ✓ ✓	$750
Thomas FC3	3/28/18 ✓	Adjourned ✓ ✓	
Ming FC7	11/15/18 ✓	Trial ✓ ✓	X
Thomas FC3	5/16/17 ✓	Dismissed ✓ ✓	
Ming FC7	3/6/18 ✓	Trial ✓ ✓	$1,000
Ming FC7	5/13/18 ✓	Adjourned ✓ ✓	
Thomas FC3	7/29/18 ✓	Defaulted ✓ ✓	
Ming FC7	2/17/19 ✓	Trial ✓ ✓	$1,150
Ming FC7	2/14/19 ✓	Adjourned ✓ ✓	
Thomas FC3	5/2/19 ✓	Dismissed ✓ ✓	
Ming FC7	3/6/19 ✓	Trial ✓ ✓	X
Ming FC7	4/21/19 ✓	Adjourned ✓ ✓	

Civil Court List of Cases On the Court Calendar Nov. 4, 2019 - November 8, 2019			
Judge Presiding	Date Case Filed	Case Disposition	Settlement Award Amount
Hawkins *CIV24*	2/5/18 ✓	Adjourned ✓ ✓	
Donato *CIV32*	6/19/17 ✓	Dismissed ✓ ✓	
Donato *CIV32*	4/2/19 ✓	Adjourned ✓ ✓	
Hawkins *CIV24*	7/21/17 ✓	Settled ✓ ✓	X
Donato *CIV32*	10/29/18 ✓	Settled ✓ ✓	$5,900
Hawkins *CIV24*	3/18/19 ✓	Adjourned ✓ ✓	
Donato *CIV32*	9/15/18 ✓	Settled ✓ ✓	$12,500
Donato *CIV32*	12/18/18 ✓	Adjourned ✓ ✓	
Hawkins *CIV24*	2/4/19 ✓	Settled ✓ ✓	X
Donato *CIV32*	2/15/19 ✓	Adjourned ✓ ✓	
Hawkins *CIV24*	5/1/19 ✓	Defaulted ✓ ✓	

Coding Table Part / Judge Presiding	
Part	Judge Presiding
CR9	Finnegan
CR12	Volter
FC3	Thomas
FC7	Ming
CIV24	Hawkins
CIV32	Donato

Summary Table 1:

Case Status	Cases on Calendar Nov. 4, 2019 - November 8, 2019			
	Criminal	Family	Civil	Total Cases
Adjourned	III 3	IIII 4	IIIII 5	12
Defaulted	I 1	I 1	I 1	3
Dismissed	I 1	II 2	I 1	4
Settled - with Money Award			II 2	2
Settled - no money award			II 2	2
Trial with Fine Imposed	III 3			3
Trial with no fine imposed	IIII 4			4
Trial with Restitution Ordered		III 3		3
Trial with no Restitution Ordered		II 2		2
Total Cases	12	12	11	35
Cases by Date Filed				
2017	III 3	II 2	II 2	7
2018	IIII 4	IIIII 5	IIII 4	13
2019	IIIII 5	IIIII 5	IIIII 5	15
Total Cases	12	12	11	35

(Note that in the above table only certain case status' are included.)

Summary Table 2:

Part Code	Case Status at End of Day			Settled Money Award	Trial with Fine Imposed	Trial with Restitution Ordered
	Adjourned	Defaulted	Dismissed			
CIV32 Donato	III 3		I 1	II 2		
CIV24 Hawkins	II 2	I 1				
FC7 Ming	III 3					III 3
FC3 Thomas	I 1	I 1	II 2			
CR12 Volter	I 1	I 1	I 1		I 1	
CR9 Finnegan	II 2				II 2	

Steps for filling-in Summary Table 1 and Summary Table 2:

Suggestions for Summary Table 1

1. In Summary Table 2, write next to each Judge name the Part code (from the Coding Table).

2. Starting with the "Criminal Court List of Cases On the Court Calendar", go down one row at a time and record (by placing a "ı" mark) the case status information of each case in Summary Table 1. After you have posted each "Case Disposition" from the "Criminal

Court List of Cases On the Court Calendar," place a check mark (✓) after the notation in the "Case Disposition" column in the "Criminal Court List of Cases On the Court Calendar." Do this for every row so that you will not skip a row or post a row twice.

3. After you have completed step 2, use the same "Criminal Court List of Cases On the Court Calendar", and go down one row at a time and record the year the case was filed in the bottom section of Summary Table 1. After you have posted the year the case was filed for each row, place a check mark (✓) after the notation in the "Date Case Filed" column. Do this for every row.

4. Next, repeat steps 2 and 3 using the "Family Court List of Cases On the Court Calendar" and post the case disposition and Date Year Filed to Summary Table 1.

5. Next, repeat steps 2 and 3 using the "Civil Court List of Cases On the Court Calendar" and post the case disposition and Date Year filed to Summary Table 1.

6. After you have posted all the information to Summary Table 1 (that is, you have competed entering the information in the three columns: Criminal, Family and Civil columns), fill-in the "Total Cases" column and two rows.

Suggestions for Summary Table 2

As we discussed, this summary table lists the "Part" (courtroom) where each Judge presides. To "tie-in" or "correlate" the name of the Judge in the "Criminal", "Family", and "Civil" tables, we wrote the Code next to the name of each Judge (column 1). By doing this, we can easily post the information to Summary Table 2. If we have time, we can also write the code next to each judge's name in the first three tables.

As we go down each row and post the disposition of each case, we place another check mark after the case disposition in the three tables. (See completed Summary Table 2.)

Note that in Summary Table 2 only some dispositions are listed. If a case has a disposition not listed in Table 2, then we did not post that information.

Questions 61-75

61. The total number of Adjourned case for the three courts is:
    A. 6
    B. 8
    C. 10
    D. 12 (Criminal 3 + Family 4 + Civil 5 = 12).

62. What is the total number of cases for the three courts?
    A. 30
    B. 35 (Criminal 12 + Family 12 + Civil 11 = 35).
    C. 36
    D. 34

63. The Judge who has code FC3 is Judge_____.

   A. Ming

   B. Thomas

   C. Finnegan

   D. Hawkins

64. The number of Adjourned Cases for all three courts exceeded the total number of Dismissed Cases for all three courts by _____.

   A. 6

   B. 7

   C. 8 (Adjourned 12 - Dismissed 4 = 8.)

   D. 10

65. The greatest total number of cases filed in all three courts in one year is:

   A. 7

   B. 15 (2019)

   C. 35

   D. 13

66. The Judge that had the greatest number of dismissed cases is Judge_____.

   A. Donato

   B. Volter

   C. Thomas (2)

   D. Ming

67. The number of cases that were "Settled With Money Award" is ___.

   A. 1
   B. 2 (Judge Donato)
   C. 3
   D. 4

68. The two Judges that tied for the greatest number of adjourned cases are Judges _____ and Judge _____.

   A. Donato and Hawkins
   B. Hawkins and Ming
   C. Ming and Finnegan
   D. Donato and Ming (3 each)

69. The total number of cases filed in 2017 plus 2019 is ___.

   A. 20
   B. 21
   C. 22 (7 + 15 = 22)
   D. 24

70. How many cases had the disposition "Trial With No Fine Imposed"?

   A. 4
   B. 3
   C. 2
   D. 1

71. How many Family Court cases were filed in 2018?
   A. 1
   C. 5
   B. 3
   D. 7

72. What is the total of Criminal Court adjourned cases plus Family Court dismissed cases?
   A. 2
   C. 3
   B. 5 (3 + 2)
   D. 4

73. What is the total number of cases disposed by "Trial With Fine Imposed" by Judges Volter and Finnegan?
   A. 2
   B. 5
   C. 3 (1 + 2)
   D. 4

74. The total number of dismissed cases in all three courts exceeds the total number of defaulted cases by ____.
   A. 1 (4 - 3)
   C. 3
   B. 2
   D. 7

75. Which three Judges did not have any "Defaulted" cases?
   A. Hawkins, Ming and Finnegan
   B. Donato, Thomas and Ming
   C. Ming, Volter and Hawkins
   D. Donato, Ming and Finnegan

End of Practice Test

Practice Test Answer Key

1. B	26. B	51. B
2. D	27. D	52. A
3. D	28. B	53. A
4. B	29. C	54. A
5. C	30. C	55. B
6. A	31. D	56. C
7. B	32. C	57. D
8. A	33. D	58. A
9. B	34. A	59. B
10. B	35. D	60. A
11. C	36. D	61. D
12. B	37. C	62. B
13. B	38. D	63. B
14. C	39. D	64. C
15. A	40. C	65. B
16. B	41. C	66. C
17. D	42. A	67. B
18. B	43. B	68. D
19. B	44. D	69. C
20. C	45. C	70. A
21. D	46. D	71. C
22. B	47. A	72. B
23. B	48. B	73. C
24. D	49. C	74. A
25. B	50. C	75. D

Made in United States
North Haven, CT
13 August 2025

71656352R00075